Brazilian Mythology

Enthralling Folktales, Vibrant Folklore, Mythical Legends, and Deities of Brazil

© Copyright 2024 - All rights reserved.

The content contained within this book may not be reproduced, duplicated, or transmitted without direct written permission from the author or the publisher.

Under no circumstances will any blame or legal responsibility be held against the publisher, or author, for any damages, reparation, or monetary loss due to the information contained within this book, either directly or indirectly.

Legal Notice:

This book is copyright protected. It is only for personal use. You cannot amend, distribute, sell, use, quote, or paraphrase any part, or the content within this book, without the consent of the author or publisher.

Disclaimer Notice:

Please note the information contained within this document is for educational and entertainment purposes only. All effort has been executed to present accurate, up-to-date, reliable, and complete information. No warranties of any kind are declared or implied. Readers acknowledge that the author is not engaging in the rendering of legal, financial, medical, or professional advice. The content within this book has been derived from various sources. Please consult a licensed professional before attempting any techniques outlined in this book.

By reading this document, the reader agrees that under no circumstances is the author responsible for any losses, direct or indirect, that are incurred as a result of the use of the information contained within this document, including, but not limited to, errors, omissions, or inaccuracies.

Free limited time bonus

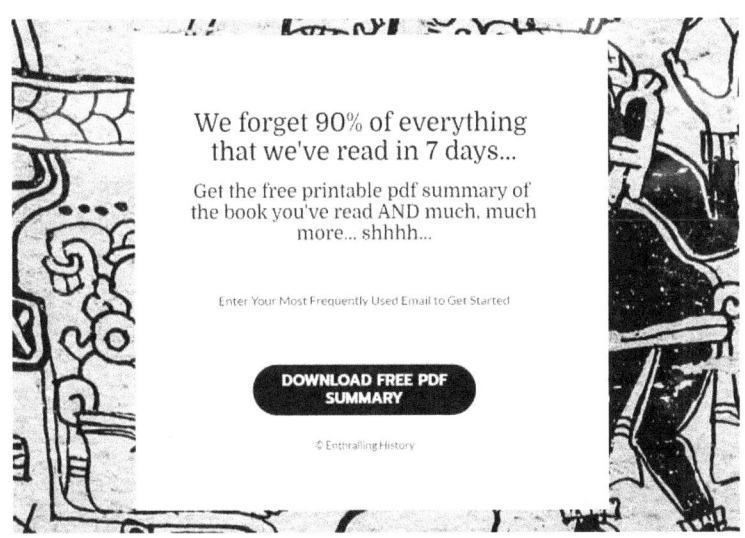

Stop for a moment. We have a free bonus set up for you. The problem is this: we forget 90% of everything that we read after 7 days. Crazy fact, right? Here's the solution: we've created a printable, 1-page pdf summary for this book that you're reading now. All you have to do to get your free pdf summary is to go to the following website: https://livetolearn.lpages.co/enthrallinghistory/

Or, Scan the QR code!

Once you do, it will be intuitive. Enjoy, and thank you!

Table of Contents

INTRODUCTION 1
CHAPTER ONE - THE CREATION MYTHS...5
CHAPTER TWO - HIGH SPIRITS 17
CHAPTER THREE - RIVER MYTHS...26
CHAPTER FOUR - JAGUAR TALES 32
CHAPTER FIVE - MONSTROUS BEASTS 39
CHAPTER SIX - SERPENTS, SNAKES, AND WORMS 48
CHAPTER SEVEN - BRAZILIAN BOGEYMEN..55
CHAPTER EIGHT -AFRICAN INFLUENCES 61
CHAPTER NINE - FOLKTALES AND FAIRYTALES 67
CONCLUSION 73
HERE'S ANOTHER BOOK BY ENTHRALLING HISTORY THAT YOU MIGHT LIKE..77
FREE LIMITED TIME BONUS..78
FURTHER READING..79

Introduction

Most of northern Brazil, approximately 40 percent of the country, is veined by the Amazon Basin. The Amazon River, which flows from west to east from the Andes, runs through eight countries but mostly through Brazil and Peru. The river ends in the Atlantic Ocean at Marajó Bay, Brazil. The Amazon River has the largest volume of water of any river in the world and the biggest drainage system. This vast, extensive region is roughly 2.72 million square miles (6.9 million square kilometers) in size, and the climate is tropical and hot (around 70 to 90°F or 21 to 32°C) with a high volume of rainfall (60 to 200 inches or 150 to 500 centimeters) year-round.

Two-thirds of the Amazon Basin is covered with vast forests of lush, hardwood trees. In the Amazon rainforest, more than forty thousand plant species grow. There are 2.5 million different insect species, 3,000 fish species, some 1,300 bird species, and 427 types of mammals. It is the most biologically diverse place on Earth.

The Amazon rainforest is sometimes referred to as the "lungs of the earth," and for good reason. The lush and diverse flora takes in carbon dioxide and emits at least 6 percent of the world's oxygen. (Historically, the figure was much greater—20 percent—but recent studies suggest photosynthetic organisms that live in the ocean provide a larger proportion of oxygen in the earth's atmosphere than had been originally understood.)

The heavy, wide crowns of the immensely tall trees (many of them measuring 150 to 200 feet or 45 to 60 meters) form the closed canopy that shields the forest from most of the sunlight. Their branches provide habitats for tree frogs, snakes, monkeys (including the buffy-headed marmoset and the crested capuchin, which are indigenous only to Brazil), an incredible range of birds, and invertebrates, including spiders and insects (beetles, moths, bees, wasps, ants, termites, and butterflies). Although the rainforest soil is relatively poor, it provides perfect conditions for alligators, larger snakes like anacondas and boa constrictors, and animals like capybaras, jaguars, and sloths.

In the slow-flowing river channels and lakes, there are manatees, freshwater dolphins, and turtles, although their numbers have been seriously depleted due to being hunted for their meat. There are also several species of piranhas and electric eels. This rich and diverse flora and fauna, so much of it unique to the region, has given rise to many stories and myths throughout the ages.

The very discovery of the Amazon by Europeans was the result of chasing an elusive myth. Francisco de Orellana, a Spanish conquistador and explorer who had assisted his cousin, Francisco Pizarro, in taking possession of Peru, set out on an expedition led by Pizarro's half-brother to explore the regions to the east of Quito. In April 1542, he took a two-masted sailing ship ahead of the main party for provisions and reached the junction of the Napo and Marañón Rivers. Realizing it would be foolhardy to attempt to return due to the current, he drifted with the tide until he reached the mouth of the Amazon in August. When he finally returned to Spain (after a brief sojourn in Trinidad), he had remarkable stories to tell.

He spoke of El Dorado, which is thought to be a reference to the ancient culture of the Muisca people, who offered copious quantities of gold to a lagoon near Bogotá, Colombia, during inauguration ceremonies for new chiefs. The newly appointed chief sailed across the blue waters on a golden raft covered in honey and gold dust, which must have been quite a spectacle if Orellana really witnessed it.

Orellana also told of an attack by a tribe of warrior women that resembled the fabled Amazons of classical Greek literature. They might have been a beardless tribe firing at the ship from the banks of the river at a distance; he and his men just mistook them for women.

Orellana was keen to return to make another exploration of this huge river that had become known as the Amazon after the mythical Greek tribe, but Spain and Portugal were in a bitter dispute over ownership of the lands. The king refused to fund such a voyage but offered some unofficial assistance. Orellana's return to South America was a disaster from the start. He lost ships and men crossing the Atlantic from Spain, and when he finally returned to the Amazon, his ship capsized, and he drowned.

Rumors of a wonderful city of gold captured the interest of European explorers, who were already enamored with the new and exotic South American lands. They scrambled to make expeditions in Colombia, Venezuela, Guyana, and northern Brazil, promising the possibility of immense wealth to their patrons. Sir Walter Raleigh made two such voyages for Queen Elizabeth I of England, and Iberian conquistadors continued their searches, but no such city was ever found. It wasn't until the beginning of the 19th century that the rumor was finally dismissed as a myth.

Even the name Brazil may stem from a myth. Pedro Álvares Cabral, the first European to lead an expedition to Brazil, named the region Ilha de Vera Cruz ("Island of the True Cross") in 1500. It was later discovered that the region was not an island, and it began to be known as Terra de Santa Cruz ("Land of the Holy Cross"). It began to be called Brazil sometime in the 16th century. This name was derived from the redwood tree *paubrasilia*. Its crimson timber was said to be the color of *brasa* (Latin for "embers") and proved a strong wood able to bear heavy loads. It was also known for being particularly attractive. It quickly became an extremely valuable resource, and the wood was shipped back to Portugal for building and for the red dye that could be extracted from its bark.

However, there has been some suggestion (namely in an essay by the author J. R. R. Tolkien) that the country of Brazil might have been named after the mythical and elusive island of Hy-Brasil. It is supposedly only visible through the mists every seven years and is said to be somewhere west of Ireland in the Atlantic Ocean, but this has been dismissed as a fanciful thought by etymologists.

The modern country of Brazil is the fifth largest in the world after Russia, China, Canada, and the United States. It covers a massive area, so it should come as no surprise that it was home to many different tribal groups. It is estimated that when Cabral and his fleet chanced upon Brazil, some two thousand tribes, between two and five million people, lived there. Most of them were semi-nomadic, and they lived in coastal areas or by rivers where fish were plentiful, and they could cultivate plants for food.

It is believed their ancestors originally migrated fifteen thousand years earlier from Asia over the Bering Strait. From there, they gradually moved south through North America. Over the years, the indigenous people began to form myths about the land around them. As the centuries passed, these myths transformed due to colonization, conversion to Christianity, and slavery. European ideas, particularly religion, impacted the characters found in ancient tales. Different messages would be told, and the newer generations passed on the altered version, with the original often being lost to time.

Today, Brazil is seen as a creative, vibrant country with a strong identity despite its population being of such diverse heritage. It is a country associated with sports, particularly football or soccer, samba, carnivals, cuisine, and literature.

Brazil's outstanding literary tradition carries on what was done by the ancient settlers. In recent times, it tends to deal with themes of social and racial injustice. Elements from the country's rich mythology are referenced and echoed in poetry and novels crafted by writers who are familiar with these traditions.

Chapter One – The Creation Myths

Brazilian stories of how the world and humanity came to be are as varied and diverse as its people and landscapes. Some of these myths are lost, incomplete, or have been changed through the ages, but those that remain give a fascinating insight into Brazilian cultures and communities.

The Tupi people inhabited some three-quarters of the coastal regions of Brazil when the Portuguese arrived at the beginning of the 16th century. They were accomplished farmers and grew a variety of vegetables and legumes. Although they were divided into numerous individual tribes, ranging from three hundred to two thousand people, they shared a common language. The Portuguese settlers found the Tupi to have no discernible religion, but there were myths and legends that the colonizers perhaps overlooked in their enthusiasm to bring these people under the wing of Christianity.

The Tupi told stories of a god named Nhanderuvuçu. He was the principal god and the creator. He destroyed everything that had come before and then produced two souls from which he created everything: the world, the air, and the water. He unraveled chaos to bring order, which brought the other Tupi deities into being.

One of these was Tupã, the god of thunder and the skies. One day, he released two birds into the sky. One was Guaraci, the sun god. He was responsible for all living things during daylight. The other bird, Jaci, became the moon and oversaw all living things at night.

In another version, Tupã only created Guaraci. He was exhausted from endlessly overseeing the world. So, Tupã made him a sister whose lunar gleam would prevent the world from descending into complete darkness while the sun god slept. When Guaraci saw her, he was dazzled by her beauty and welcomed the opportunity to sleep so he could wake up and be captivated by her all over again.

Guaraci asked Tupã to convey his deep admiration for Jaci. Tupã formed Rudá, the god of love and affection, to take these messages to Jaci while the lovelorn sun god slept.

Jaci was in the rainforest when she finally met her brother Guaraci. She was just as mesmerized by his golden, glittering magnificence as he was with her, and as the two gazed upon each other, Guaraci's fiery passion threatened to set the earth ablaze. Jaci's tears of love and happiness almost caused the earth to flood. They realized they could never be together, so they reluctantly parted.

Feckless Guaraci soon forgot all about his lunar love since she took great care never to appear until he was asleep. However, Jaci remained heartbroken. Her tears fell to the earth and down the mountains, eventually forming the mighty Amazon River.

Jaci was the most beautiful and benevolent of all the divine beings. She was responsible for plants and reproduction. Despite her loveliness, she found herself isolated and lonely, pining for her beloved in the cool night sky. So, from time to time, she would choose a pure young woman to join her in the heavens as a star.

One girl, called Naiá, longed to join Jaci and become one of her celestial maidens. She wandered in the forest clearings and the mountains, searching for the moon in the hopes of persuading her, but she could never find her. As time passed, Naiá refused to eat. Preoccupied with her search, she began to waste away.

One evening, she awoke to see the moon reflected in a lake. As if in a dream, she threw herself into the water with her arms outstretched as if to embrace the moon and drowned.

Jaci saw what happened and was moved by the girl's sacrifice. She decided to grant her a unique honor, allowing her to live forever between the water and the skies. Naiá was made into the "water star," the Amazonian water lily (*Victoria amazonica* or *Vitória-Régia*), a giant white flower that lasts just forty-eight hours. It opens its milky white petals on the first night and then changes color to a purplish red when it opens again on the second night. This is Naiá opening her arms to bathe in the moon's light.

In the period when day turns into night, women traditionally ask Jaci to protect their men who leave on nocturnal hunting trips. She encourages these hunters to hurry home to their wives by reawakening their love for them while they are away. In some versions of this story, the god of love, Rudá, was accompanied by Cairé, the full moon, and Caitití, the new moon. These were the times when lovers should unite.

The Tupi god of the underworld was Anhangá, who was also the protector of animals. Ceuci was the goddess of the fields and dwellings, and Sumé was the god of agriculture and discipline.

The Guaraní people are another indigenous group in South America. They are distinguished from the Tupi people by their use of the Guaraní language and were more prominent in the southern regions of Brazil, Paraguay, Argentina, and Bolivia. Their creation myth begins with Tupã being married to the moon goddess Arasy. With her help, he came down to Earth to create everything: the seas, the rivers, the forests, and the mountains. Next came all living things and, finally, Tau, the spirit of evil, and Angatupyry, the spirit of goodness.

The first humans created by Tupã were Rupave and Sypave. Tupã was good to them and helped them learn essential life skills, such as hunting, building shelters, and how certain plants could be used to eat or heal. He encouraged them to have many children together. Their second son, Marangatú, became a great leader of humankind. He had a beautiful daughter named Kerana. When the evil spirit Tau saw the lovely Kerana, he was determined to have her. So, he transformed himself into a handsome stranger in order to seduce her. However, when he arrived at her home, Angatupyry was waiting for him, having realized his ill intent.

For seven days, the good and evil spirits battled until Tau was defeated, and good prevailed. Pytajovái, the god of valor and warriors, exiled him. All seemed well until evil Tau returned in the dead of night and abducted Kerana.

Together, Tau and Kerana had seven sons, but Arasy was appalled at Kerana's abduction and cursed all of them. They became hideous beings. The oldest was Teju Jagua, a giant lizard with seven dog heads whose eyes burned with fire. Tupã managed to tame him and made him the spirit of caves. He only ate fruit and honey and lived a quiet life, guarding treasure found in caverns. Teju Jagua was almost immobile because of the weight of his many dog heads. He rolled around in his dark subterranean dwellings so that fragments of gold, silver, and colored gems stuck to his scaly skin.

The second son, Mbói Tu'ĩ ("snake parrot"), became a huge serpent with a parrot's head and a blood-red forked tongue. His head was covered with feathers, and his violent squawk could be heard from miles away. Anyone who came across him was destined for bad luck. He became the protector of all aquatic creatures and swamplands.

Moñái, the third son of Tau and Kerana, became the god of the air and open fields. He had the writhing body of a snake and two antennae-like horns on his head. His gaze was mesmerizing and hypnotic, and he coiled around trees to capture birds, which he ate.

Jasy Jateré, the fourth son, is often described as a sort of goblin or gnome. His name means "small piece of moon," and this was manifested in his lustrous pale hair. He had startling blue eyes and often carried a magical staff. He wore a hat, but he was naked otherwise. His hat enhanced his powers, which were unpleasant and disturbing. He whistled like a bird to attract children, and then he kidnapped them. He would take them to a remote mountain area where he played with them and fed them honey or sweet fruits. Then, as he prepared to leave them, he licked or kissed them, leaving them deaf, suffering seizures, or giving them some other long-term debilitating condition. In some versions, he preferred to drown the unfortunate child. The Guaraní people said he could be rendered helpless if he was plied with drink and if his staff was taken from him. If this happened, he would sob pitifully, just like one of the children he had lured away.

In other versions of Jasy Jateré's story, he searches for children who will not take a nap. As such, he was made the spirit of the siesta and guardian of the yerba mate, a plant native to South America that can be steeped in water to make a drink comparable to tea. This drink was extremely popular with the Guaraní and some Tupi communities before the colonization of the region. In these tales, Jasy Jateré was a useful cautionary villain for warning children who refused to take their afternoon nap.

Kurupi, the fifth son, was the spirit of fertility, sexuality, and lust. Another short being with a human-like appearance, he was hairy and ugly and had an extremely long penis. His penis was so long that he had to wind it around his waist several times like a belt. He was often found lurking in the forest, his movements clumsy and ungainly, perhaps due to the discomfort of his bizarre deformity. He would assault any woman who dared to walk there alone. She would be left dead or pregnant after his attentions. At nighttime, he dared to steal into villages. His penis was able to negotiate its way through doors, windows, and other openings, allowing him to find a way to sleeping women whom he impregnated.

Many unexplained pregnancies (unmarried women and some who had not had relations with their husbands) were blamed on Kurupi. Children he was supposed to have fathered were expected to resemble him. They would be short, dark, ugly, and hairy. Sometimes, children who fit that description were teased, with others saying they were Kurupi's sons or daughters.

The most violent and savage son, Ao Ao, was a sheeplike creature with huge claws and enormous fangs, which he used to tear into human flesh. He has also been compared to a peccary, the porcine South American mammal that can be more aggressive than a sheep, especially when protecting its territory or young. Ao Ao was named after the dreadful howl he made, which alerted people to his presence. Once he had honed in on a victim, the only way to escape was to climb one of the palm trees sacred to the Guaraní.

Ao Ao was fed children abducted by his brother Jasy Jateré from time to time, and he is also associated with reproduction, as he fathered several children.

The seventh and youngest son, Luison (or sometimes Lobizón), was a kind of wolf man. In his earliest incarnation, he represented death since he feasted on rotting meat and skulked around burial grounds and cemeteries. If one felt the cold touch of his paw, they would die soon after.

Fortunately for the Guaraní people, they did not need to fear this foul family forever. These seven brothers had a story about their demise. The third of the brothers, the serpent Moñái, was a very crafty thief. He robbed villages and hid his spoils in a cave. The communities he stole from blamed one another for his raids and bitterly fought against each other until they realized who the real thief was. A beautiful young woman, Porâsí, offered to help put an end to his misdemeanors and his vile brothers at the same time. She flirted with Moñái and managed to persuade him that she had fallen in love with him. Before they could marry, she asked to meet his brothers.

She stayed with Teju Jagua as Moñái went to gather his brothers for the ceremony. When they all reunited in the oldest brother's cave, Porâsí ensured each of them had plenty to drink. Soon, they were completely inebriated. She tried to sneak away with the intention of sealing the cave shut with a large stone, leaving the horrible brothers inside, but Moñái grabbed her. She screamed to alert the people waiting outside with the great stone and told them to close the cave with her inside, sacrificing herself.

The monstrous sons of Tau and Kerana were no more. Angatupyry raised the soul of the courageous Porâsí from the dark cave where she had died and made her into the morning star to remind the people of her sacrifice.

The Xingu people, who today inhabit part of Mato Grosso, a state in central Brazil to the south of the Amazon rainforest, tell a sad story about the creation of the first man, Mavutsinim, who lived all alone. He was desperately lonely until he transformed a shell (or a clam) into a woman and married her. In time, they had a son. Mavutsinim took him away to travel and hunt with him. The boy's mother was devastated. She wept inconsolably and returned to her lagoon to become a shell again. This story is often viewed as an allegory for the circle of life, particularly for women. She is born, leaves the family home for marriage and motherhood, feels a great loss when her children grow and leave the home, and then eventually dies. Mavutsinim's thoughtlessness or cruelty toward his shell-wife is a portent of the misogyny women faced in less enlightened ages.

In the state of Pará, located in northern Brazil, the indigenous Arará people speak of Akuanduba, their creator. He existed at a time when the sky and water were separated only by a small shell. At that time, humans were the stars in the sky and led a simple existence eating, drinking, and sleeping. Whenever these star people began to eat, drink, or sleep to excess, they would upset the natural balance, and Akuanduba would play his magical flute so order could be restored.

Because humans lack self-discipline and common sense and cannot see what is best for them, this peaceful existence came to an end when the star people selfishly started stealing from one another. This escalated into so much rage and resentment they could not, or rather would not, hear the conciliatory notes from Akuanduba's flute. The sky broke, and the moon and all of the star people fell into the water.

The elderly star folk and the young children drowned or died from the impact of the fall. The birds were alarmed to see this disaster unfold, and a curica (a parrot) managed to get hold of the moon and dragged it back into the heavens. A small indentation said to be left by its beak can still be seen on the moon's surface at times. Parrots swooped over the water, picked up some of the surviving people, and returned them to the skies, where they continued to exist as stars.

However, the water was full of evil spirits, and the surviving people began to experience misery that they had never experienced as stars under Akuanduba's guardianship. He had lost interest in helping them and had transformed himself into a terrible black jaguar that stalked the people.

Eventually, the people managed to form a community with help from the creatures of the land. The sloths taught them to feast, and the macaws stole fire for them. They discovered the edible animals and plants in the forest and learned how to build and weave. They even made flutes so they could make music and sing like they had when they were stars in the sky.

The Arará developed into great warriors and hunters, and they always remained grateful and respectful toward the birds that saved them. The name Arará means "people of the red macaws" (the Tupi word for macaw is *arà*).

The Yanomami indigenous ethnic group from the northern region of the state of Amazonas speak of a birdlike god named Omam (or Omai) who created the world. He maintained and repaired it by adding layers of nature, such as the clouds, the sky, and the seas. When he was satisfied, he went fishing in the ocean to appreciate what he had made. There, he found a woman. When he had "freed" her sexual organs using piranha teeth, he made her the mother of all the people.

The Baniwa people, who live by the Içana River on the borders of Brazil, Colombia, and Venezuela, have an extremely complex myth about the origin of the world. At the beginning of time, the earth was very small, and all of the animals and people lived in chaos. The animals were wild and savage. One day, the Lord of All the Animals devoured one of the people and then tossed one of its finger bones into the river.

An old woman related to this person wept so bitterly for her loss that the Lord of All the Animals (sometimes called Enumhere) allowed her to go and get this bone. Inside it were three tiny shrimp called the Nhiãperikuli ("He inside the bone"). The old woman took the bone to her home and nurtured it. The shrimp transformed into crickets. As she fed them, they started to sing and grow. Under her care, they grew larger each day and eventually developed into humans.

These Nhiãperikuli began to change the world. They introduced order, and when they were ready, they took vengeance on the wild animals that had devoured the old woman's family.

The Lord of All the Animals was furious with this new world, but he slyly concealed his true feelings and asked the brothers to help him establish a garden. While they were surveying the area, he set fire to the edges of the land. Soon, there was a huge blaze. Each brother bored a hole into one of the embaúba trees and got inside them. When the flames reached these trees, they exploded, and the Nhiãperikuli flew into the air. This made them immortal.

The three brothers had a son together named Kuwai. His body was full of holes and encased all of the natural elements of the world. Amaru, the "first" woman (the old woman who nurtured the Nhiãperikuli apparently didn't count), appeared at around the same time.

Inside Kuwai was everything that makes the world as it is, the sights, sounds, smells, and tastes. As these things were released from him, the world grew into its actual size. As well as populating the earth with every known element—spirits, animals, diseases, songs, and the sounds of the forest—he turned to the people and explained the nature of existence to them.

At this point, this common origin story becomes intertwined with the myth of another major character of Brazilian mythology, Jurupari. However, in the Baniwa people's tradition, Kuwai turned into a monster to devour three disobedient boys who had broken their initiation process by eating roasted nuts. Afterward, the Nhiãperikuli pushed Kuwai into an inferno, which made the earth contract into its smaller size again.

The shamans, or *pajé*, of the region recount that this was by no means the end of Kuwai. He retreated to the center of the world to become the Lord of Sickness. All of the diseases, illnesses, and poor health conditions generated from his earthly remains and poisoned the environment. His spirit body was covered in thick black fur like the sloth. When he encountered the souls of the sick, he encased them in his arms—in the same manner as the sloth—and squeezed the breath from them as the *pajés* frantically negotiated with him in the hope he would allow their unfortunate patient to continue living.

From the ashes of the huge fire that had destroyed the physical presence of Kuwai, the people found sacred pipes and trumpets. The Nhiãperikuli directed the men to play these instruments in sacred ceremonies, but the women grew envious and stole them. As they fled, they played the pipes, and the world opened up again. Nhiãperikuli and the men, in the form of wild animals, hunted them down to take back the instruments.

Afterward, the Nhiãperikuli produced a group of people from the Aiari River. These would be the ancestors of the human race.

The universe, in this Baniwa myth system, is divided into multiple layers, from four (Wapinakwa, "The Place of Bones," Hekwapi, "This World," Apakwa Hekwapi, "The Other World," and Apakwa Eenu, "The Sky of the Other World") to twenty-five: twelve above the human plain and twelve below. Kuwai is placed (by the *pajé*) with the other spirits they share contact with, such as the bird spirits that help them to find lost souls somewhere in Apakwa Eenu.

The Nhiãperkuli remained the supreme being. They were responsible for the heart of the world and existed in Dio, a heavenly plain where there is no suffering or sickness. With them lives Kamathawa, the harpy eagle, a symbol that has come to represent shamans and *pajé* throughout South America.

Kamathawa is regarded as a sentinel tasked with guarding Nhiãperkuli's wisdom and sacred medicine knowledge held in crystals. In traditional ceremonies, *pajé* use harpy eagle feathers to sweep and clear the skies in order to see into these crystals and influence the weather when the rainy season becomes excessive.

Some people believe Kamathawa is the younger brother of the Nhiãperkuli and that he was killed by some malevolent beings. As they prepared to eat his body (having turned it into a large catfish), the Nhiãperkuli turned into a wasp and managed to retrieve Kamathawa's heart, which it cooked. As the boiling water bubbled and foamed, hawks began to fly out of it, each larger than the one before. Finally, the great harpy eagle emerged and flew in circles overhead.

The Nhiãperkuli gave this eagle Kamathawa great logs to carry. After regaining his strength, he avenged himself by killing and eating the enemies who had killed him in his previous form.

The Desana (or Dessana) people from the Rio Negro Basin believed all humans were descended from one being, Yebá Bëló, the "grandmother of the universe." She appeared from nowhere and lived in a marvelous glowing structure made from quartz. Other tribal myths describe her creating the sun and people from her chewed ipadu leaves (the leaves of the coca, a herbal plant used as a stimulant and in medicine). In another version, she took a tobacco seed from her left breast and fertilized it with milk from her right breast to form the earth.

She created five thunder men who were supposed to make the first human beings, but when they failed, Yebá Bëló made Yebá Gõãmu, the "Great Grandson of the World" and then his brother, Umukomahsu Boreka.

The two set off with the third thunder man to create humankind. The thunder man transformed himself into a serpent and slipped into the Lake of Milk until he reached the bottom. Then, as a canoe, he took the brothers to this enchanted place, and they took all the precious things they could find in the world. They built dwellings, and their precious things transformed into people. Yebá Gõãmu breathed life into them. The thunder man directed these first men to go and take a leaf from the ipadu tree and eat it. When they felt pain in their bellies, they were told to light a fire stick and dip it in a gourd of water before drinking it. Then, they should vomit in a very specific place. Once this had been completed, the first men saw they had produced two beautiful women. These people would be the common ancestors of all humanity.

The thunder man's canoe carried all of the people who had been created to the surface of the lake. They stepped onto land near a waterfall. Yebá Gõãmu remained on the canoe to create the chiefs of the first six tribes, including Boreka, the chief of the Desana. He gave each of them certain powers and enchanted treasures so that their people would live harmoniously as neighbors.

Tellingly, the seventh being he created was the white man, born with a rifle in his hand. Yebá Gõãmu did not give him any other gifts—he said he had no need of them. Yebá Gõãmu knew he was fearless and ruthless and that he would start wars in order to steal what he wanted from others. As this white man left the lake, he fired his gun and, without looking back, set off toward the sun, ready to take whatever he wanted by force.

The Kamayurá, from the northeast of Brazil near the mouth of the Amazon, relate how there was no light at the beginning, as the sun's rays were limited to the kingdom of birds in the sky. The people who existed on the earth lived in eternal darkness until the sun god, Kuat, wondered why his glorious light didn't benefit everyone.

The moon god, Iae, told him it was because Urubutsin, the two-headed king of the vultures, had taken possession of it and knitted the tree canopies together so tightly that he could keep it exclusively for the birds.

Kuat and Iae resolved to trick Urubutsin, and they persuaded the king of the flies to take the effigy of a body to the banks of the Amazon and fill it with maggots. The buzzing of the flies gained the notice of Urubutsin. Looking down from his lofty perch, he could see the effigy had bright, gleaming eyes. He and his subjects flew down to investigate, and upon finding the juicy maggots, they gorged on them with relish.

Kuat and Iae had hidden themselves in the effigy of another body. When Urubutsin approached it, they grabbed hold of his foot and refused to let go. All of Urubutsin's cowardly subjects quickly flew away, leaving him with little option but to negotiate for his freedom. After some discussion, a deal was agreed. The light would be shared, but each evening, darkness would prevail, and the moon would watch over the world.

A creation myth that came from the African Candomblé religion, which was brought to Brazil by West African enslaved people and intermingled with Christianity, is the story of Iemanjá.

This tale begins in a world of perpetual light. There was no sunrise or sunset, no nocturnal creatures, or no cool nighttime. There was only hot, bright sunlight.

The goddess Iemanjá lived deep in the sea. One of her daughters fell in love with one of the men who lived on the land and left her mother to marry him. At first, she was very happy and loved her husband and her glittering new surroundings. But after some time, the endless glare of the sun became too much for her and made her eyes hurt and her head ache. She longed to go back to her mother, where the dark, cool waters would soothe her.

Her husband was very concerned to see his wife so unhappy and sick. So, when she told him of Iemanjá's kingdom, he sent three of his men to beg the goddess for some of the cool darkness for his wife.

The men traveled the perilous journey under the water and finally reached Iemanjá's realm. They prostrated themselves before her, begging for some of the darkness their master's wife craved. As soon as the goddess realized her daughter was suffering, she gave them a large bag of her underwater darkness and told them to take it to her quickly but warned them not to open it because she had filled it with night spirits. Only her daughter would be able to control them.

The three men dragged the bag through the water and onto the land. Once there, the bag began to make strange sounds. As they carried it on their heads, they began to grow frightened. The night spirits' screeches and howls were like nothing they had heard before.

The first man was so terrified he could not stop shaking. The second suggested they should just dump the bag somewhere and run away. The third man suggested if they had a quick peek inside the bag, they would see what was making the dreadful noises and wouldn't be afraid anymore. He carefully unsealed the bag, but before he could take a look, all of the night insects, birds, and creatures swarmed out of it, and the stars sprang into the sky.

The men fled in panic, but fortunately, Iemanjá's daughter was waiting on the shore. She greeted the night spirits. Darkness descended everywhere, and the creatures calmed their noises until there was just a gentle hum. The world felt cool and soft and gleamed in the moonlight.

Iemanjá's daughter fell asleep and awoke feeling soothed and well again. Her husband was delighted to see his wife happy. As nighttime had been established in her new home, Iemanjá's daughter bestowed three gifts to the people of the land. The first was the morning star, so they might see when the night was ending. She then gave the rooster the task of calling each dawn to greet daylight. Finally, the birds agreed they would sing their most beautiful songs each morning to celebrate each new day. This period of the early morning when the sun rises became known as *madrugada*, a special time of renewal and refreshment.

Chapter Two – High Spirits

Many of the indigenous people of Brazil share stories of spirits, apparitions of people who have passed into another world after death or are the essence that makes up the very soul of humans or animals. It is, in some ways, a catch-all term that can include gods, ghosts, and entities with powers beyond the wit and understanding of men and women. Spirits are good, bad, or both at the same time. Sometimes, they are even beyond such arbitrary concepts. A good example of this is the Jurupari cult, which is found among nearly all the indigenous people of northwestern Amazonia and is known by several names, including Yurupary and Kowai. It is particularly prevalent in the Arawakan communities of the Rio Negro and the Uaupés River.

The Tupi Guaraní goddess of crops and dwellings, Ceuci, was originally a lovely young woman who lived in a village where a special tree grew. Tupã had given strict instructions that the women who lived there were forbidden from eating its fruit during their fertile periods.

Ceuci was resting in the shade of the tree one hot day and could not resist trying one of its succulent mapati, a sweet, juicy fruit rather like a grape (or a caimito or cucura, depending on the location of the story). As she bit into it, the juice ran from the flesh down her body and between her thighs.

Soon afterward, she realized she was pregnant. The elders of her community were appalled since she had no husband or partner, and they struggled to understand how she could have conceived a child. They decided to banish her from the village, so Ceuci left to have her baby on her own.

Some versions of this story are more earthy, strange, and graphic. There is the suggestion that Ceuci had been made pregnant through an incestuous relationship with an element, possibly the sun, the moon, or thunder. Since she had no vagina, the birth was only completed when she had been pierced by a particular fish.

She named her son Jurupari, and he was a remarkable, precocious boy. By the age of ten, the elders of the village who had exiled his mother listened to his ideas and recognized the wisdom of his teachings. But young Jurupari, according to different origin stories, had no mouth and existed on tobacco smoke. He was able to communicate by gestures or by making dreadful, frightening noises from holes in his body. He was not always (at least entirely) human; sometimes, he was a monkey with the head of a man or a manifestation of some kind of plant or tree.

Either way, he quickly asserted his influence and helped the people of the village understand the order of nature. He also introduced a series of rituals and rites for the men. He made it very clear that no woman should witness these sacred ceremonies. Ceuci, his mother, could not resist spying on this ceremony even though she knew it was forbidden and punishable by death.

She stole into the village, but as soon as Jurupari and the men had assembled, Tupã sent a lightning bolt, killing her instantaneously. Jurupari was called to her, but he knew she had died because she had violated the sacred rules. He prayed to Tupã to reward her for her devotion to her son and her exemplary motherhood. Suddenly, her body appeared to be filled with light as it rose from the ground and into the heavens, where it became the brightest star in the Pleiades constellation. It remained there, Jurupari told his people sagely, to remind them to respect the laws he was introducing.

Jurupari is an unusual character in Brazilian mythology. Despite all of his promise in Ceuci's story, he is generally known as the demon of dreams and an omen of bad fortune. In some legends, he is a malevolent and evil presence that sometimes suffocates people as they struggle to awake from nightmares.

The people of the Upper Xingu recount how Jurupari overhauled the male initiation ceremony, introducing fine costumes and new rituals. The boys who were ready to join the cult were sent to collect fruit for the proceedings. Although they were warned not to eat any of them, they disobeyed these instructions and roasted and ate some of them. Jurupari was furious. He called to the heavens and created a terrible thunderstorm, during which the boys ran to find shelter in a cave they had found. Unfortunately for them, it was actually Jurupari's mouth. (In some stories, it was his anus.) Jurupari quickly devoured them all.

One of the younger and smaller boys was too late to enter the "cave." He alone survived to tell the tale. Having heard of the dreadful fate that had befallen their sons, the parents of the disobedient boys vowed to take their revenge and planned to kill Jurupari. Replete from his dinner of the young men, Jurupari had gone to rest in the mountains (or the sky), but when the villagers offered him some of the fine liquor they had distilled, he couldn't resist joining the party.

When he arrived that evening, he vomited the remains of the boys he had eaten into large baskets of fruit that had been prepared for the feast and then joined the villagers, dancing and singing while consuming copious quantities of their exotic and potent drink.

But as the sun came over the horizon, the people threw him onto a fire, knowing it was the only way they could kill him. Although he was no more (other than his nightly activities as a sleep demon), the ashes of his flesh created a whole host of unpleasantness: snakes, stinging ants, and lots of other poisonous creatures. The ashes of his skeleton also brought forth the paxiúba palm, the huge "walking tree" that appears to rise from its exposed, tentacle-like roots.

Pipes were crafted from these roots, and the haunting music they produced was thenceforth Jurupari's voice. The other elements used in the rituals (such as beeswax and tobacco) were said to be his tongue, brain, and other organs.

Sometime later, the sun ordered the men to perform Jurupari's ceremony, but they were too lazy and couldn't be bothered to retrieve the paxiúba palm pipes from the water. They slept instead. The women, however, found the instruments and played the sacred music. The sun did not punish them but reversed the natural order in the village. The men did all of the work and had children, while the women dedicated themselves to Jurupari's sacred rituals.

The men found this situation untenable. They attacked the women with whips and brutalized them until they cried out in frustration. Once the men had regained control, the women were made to menstruate as a sign of their submission. It was then (at least in this version of the myth) that the sacred instrument became taboo to the womenfolk. Any woman who tried to play these instruments or even attempted to make anything similar was sentenced to death by poisoning. Once the verdict was passed, the woman was expected to take a lethal draft voluntarily, but if she refused, she was executed.

The Desana people were one of the ethnic groups that practiced the Jurupari initiation rituals that developed from this myth. In the daytime, the women and children were forbidden from entering the village longhouse while the men brought in fruits from the rainforest and played their pipes to express appreciation for nature's bountiful gifts, in particular, plentiful fish. In the evening, the music stopped, and the women were invited in to drink *yage* (ayahuasca), a traditional hallucinogenic preparation, and dance. Sometimes, the men whipped the women and children to help them grow strong and resilient.

The initiation ceremony for the young men approaching adulthood involved them being given coca leaves (the plant from which cocaine is produced), snuff, and *yage*. Then, they were whipped. When they were deemed ready, elements said to have been formed from Jurupari's ashes were gathered together to form an approximation of his body. Two men dressed in full ceremonial costume (representing Jurupari) showed them the sacred pipes. After suffering another whipping, they were taken to the river, where water was poured over their heads in a ceremony reminiscent of a baptism.

The young men must then spend several weeks completely independent from the women, learning traditional tasks exclusive to the male community, such as basket weaving and only consuming cold food and drink. This formative period ended with the young men presenting their female relatives with the baskets they had made. A festival would take place, during which these young men drank piping hot drinks and consumed hot chili peppers.

Anhangá, which means "ancient soul," is another god or spirit that is a part of several different people groups' mythologies but is inconsistent in terms of his role and purpose.

In the Tupinambá culture, Anhangá is a shapeshifter who prevents the dead from progressing to the next world. He torments and tortures the living on occasion. His presence was of the greatest concern when a recently deceased body was being prepared with the sacred rites for its journey to Guajupiá, the "Land Without Evils." Offerings were left for Anhangá beside a fire that had been lit to warm the body of the dead, as well as the food necessary for its sustenance. These fires would continue to be lit for many years by the dead's descendants to help keep those souls safe from the attention of Anhangá.

The Mawé (or Sateré) people native to the Amazon regard Anhangá as a demon with evil intent. They believe he is capable of cursing, abducting, and killing at will. Since Anhangá can take different forms, they rely on his dread of water. They think the spirits that protect the rivers help repel him.

However, in Tupi mythology, Anhangá is a genie of the forest and often appears as a mighty white stag with red eyes that burn and sharpened horns. However, he can also be an armadillo, an ox, an arapaima fish, or even a man. He vigilantly protects his habitat and punishes those who cause harm to it, especially if they harm female creatures and their young. Sometimes, he is invisible and charges at hunters, attacking them physically. Sometimes, he puts them under a spell that makes them crazy. There were rituals to keep him at bay, especially when the Tupi hunters had to go to the forest to feed their people. They left offerings (generally tobacco and liquor) or burned cashew nuts. They also made crosses with wood from the forest trees to deter Anhangá, a practice that was likely heavily influenced by the European colonizers or missionaries.

The most iconic character in Brazilian folklore is the spirit known as Saci or Saci-Pererê. He is not a god or demon; rather, he is a young Black boy with just one leg. He is always seen wearing a red cap and often smokes a pipe. He is a mischievous and cheeky entity who loves to play jokes and tricks for his own amusement.

Saci is quick despite his impairment. He juggles with burning embers, and he can ride a horse or, more often, the tropical whirlwinds known as dust devils. When he appears, cooks find their sugar has been exchanged for salt, there are flies in the soup, and milk has turned sour. Others find their most useful or treasured possessions missing and that needles have lost their sharpness. Strange, alarming animal noises can be heard in the dead of night; it is as if some horrible beast is prowling through the village.

Other people say that his whirling dancing causes the dust devils. If a rosary with each bead individually blessed is thrown into a dust devil, it might be possible to capture Saci. He will then bestow all kinds of favors and luck on his captor on the condition that he is treated well. If Saci is treated cruelly, he will become a vindictive enemy.

If throwing a rosary into a spinning tumult of dirt should prove too difficult, Saci can also be caught in a large sieve. To delay his progress, one can leave a rope full of tight and complicated knots, as this will distract him for several hours. He cannot resist unfastening them, and he will not rest until he has unpicked each and every knot.

Those wanting to endear themselves to Saci leave him gifts, usually tobacco or *cachaça*, a strong liquor made from fermented sugar cane, to avoid his attention. Anyone brave enough to steal Saci's red cap will be granted a wish, but there is a price to pay. The hat has a dreadful, pungent smell that will never leave those who have touched it.

This spirit is most likely to originate from the Ŷaci-Ŷaterê, a Tupi-Guaraní spirit, a one-legged child with eye-catching bright red hair. Just as rascally as Saci, he tricks people with animal calls and shrill whistling, but his activities are restricted to nighttime.

The enslaved African people who were brought to Brazil by the early European settlers readily took to the stories of Ŷaci-Ŷaterê. They enjoyed telling their children about this wicked little sprite who was just naughty enough to enthrall youngsters without terrifying them; life was hard enough already.

Because of this, over time, Saci developed into a Black boy. The red hair became a red cap. Since the elders of the African communities tended to be the storytellers and frequently enjoyed a reed pipe of tobacco as they held court, Saci developed his own smoking habit.

The Portuguese in Brazil compared Saci with the trasgu, a little forest goblin creature dressed in leaves and moss. He has a black face and is also a trickster. Some of Saci's antics might have been heavily influenced by him. There are also similarities to the mythological monopods, dwarf-like creatures with one oversized foot in the center of their bodies. These creatures were described in ancient Greek and Roman literature and were still thought to exist in some medieval etymologies.

As well as being vulnerable to rosary beads, Saci will stop his misbehaving and flee if he sees a crucifix, leaving behind just the faintest whiff of sulfur (an element long associated with the devil in Christian folklore).

In some stories, Saci has the power to control the weather and can appear and disappear at will; his glowing pipe can only be seen by the most observant. He cannot cross water unless he transforms himself into a *matitaperê* (or *matita pereira*), the striped cuckoo.

The classic children's book *O Saci*, written by Montero Lobato in 1921, is an enduring favorite among Brazilian children throughout the country. It tells the story of a young boy, Pedrinho, who lives on a farm in São Paulo. He learns about Saci from his grandfather. He decides to capture him to learn his secrets, and as the two engage in a battle of wits, each trying to outdo the other, they become close friends. They learn important lessons about trust, comradeship, resilience, and respect for the natural world.

A similar impish creature, mostly known in the state of Rio Grande do Sul, is the sanguanel. Although he is said to be harmless, his activities are sinister and worrisome by modern standards.

Thought to have originated from myths shared by Italian immigrants, the sanguanel is a kind of bright red hobgoblin that lives in the forests and mountainous areas. He likes to play pranks and tricks on adults, usually related to his ability to appear and disappear, but he is most interested in very young children and babies. He kidnaps them and hides with them in tall trees or shrubs. While frantic parents search for their missing children, he feeds his little captives on honey and water, which he drips into their mouths from special cups he forms from leaves. When the children are found, they are disoriented and sleepy. They can never quite recall what happened to them while they were in the sanguanel's care.

The sanguanel is supposed to have a twin sister called the sanguanela. She is his opposite in every way. Rather than being red, she has white skin and blonde hair. She prefers vinegar to wine (suggesting, perhaps, that the sanguanel enjoys his liquor) and has some power over water.

Romãozinho is the nasty spirit of a child that was once a human. He was a very bad boy from the start. He relished destroying plants and flowers. As soon as he was old enough, he hunted and killed any living creatures, even the songbirds that make life so pleasant for everyone. He hated everyone and never passed up an opportunity to spread spite, suspicion, and bad feelings. He even loathed his parents and managed to persuade his father that his innocent mother was in love with another man.

One day, his mother asked him to take his father a chicken she had cooked for him while he was working in the fields. Romãozinho ate the whole chicken while he walked. When he eventually reached his father, he handed over the chicken bones and said that was all that was left. His mother and her boyfriend had eaten the rest.

Ramãozinho's father, mad with rage, returned to the family home and struck and killed his poor wife. As she was taking her last breaths, she saw her malevolent son smiling to himself, and she realized that he was behind the terrible fate that had befallen her. Her last act was to place a terrible curse on him: he would never know heaven or hell while a single human remained on Earth.

Her son, though completely remorseless, found himself reduced to wandering the world. He is no longer human, but he plays tricks on people, mainly out of boredom and maliciousness.

It is possible that this myth is a Brazilian interpretation of Ahasvero, a cursed immortal man from 13th-century Europe. He was also left wandering aimlessly for all of time.

In the northeastern states of Brazil, especially in the Sertão area, the spirit of a young woman known as Comadre Fulozinha ("Good Friend Blossom") is said to protect the rainforest. She has long dark hair. It is so thick and lustrous that it can cover her whole body. She is tall and willowy, and she is said to wear a grey diaphanous dress and a red necklace that is so beautiful and intricate that it could not have been made by human hands.

Some communities call her *Mãe da Mata* ("Mother of the Woods") and say flowers grow wherever she has walked. She has a distinctive whistle that becomes quieter as she approaches. Anyone who hears her is advised to leave since she dislikes humans disturbing the forests.

The most common origin story says that Comadre Fulozinha was a caboclo (person of mixed indigenous Brazilian and European descent) girl, possibly the daughter of a rich, influential white man who had tricked an indigenous woman into sleeping with him. When her mother died, this girl vowed to avenge her by targeting humans, particularly men, who defiled beauty and innocence, especially in nature.

In another story, she was a little girl who became lost in the forest and died before her parents could find her.

She takes her role as the guardian of nature very seriously. If she comes across anyone vandalizing her domain, she will approach slowly, making a quiet, hissing noise before suddenly setting about them, whipping them with her braided hair or stinging vines with unexpected stamina and strength. She can be deterred, like Saci, with gifts. She prefers porridge or honey. She loves to braid and will tightly plait and weave horse tails or lengths of string with astonishing dexterity.

Comadre Fulozinha is a divine entity to the Jurema cult in Paraíba. Though her stories are not as detailed as some of the other entities in the Brazilian myths, her guardianship of nature has made her a popular character and very relevant in the awakened consciousness to preserve the planet.

Chapter Three – River Myths

The mighty Amazon is the centerpiece of the most extensive river system in the world. Other systems in Brazil, such as the Tocantins-Araguaia in the north, the São Francisco in the northeast and east, and the Paraguay-Paraná-Plata in the south, are also significant. The role of these rivers in Brazilian myths is inescapable.

The deity that is responsible for the rivers in the Brazilian pantheon is Iara, the water goddess. She is also known as Yara and Uiara, and she is originally from ancient Tupi mythology.

A mermaid-type spirit, she is usually depicted as half woman, half fish with long hair, sometimes blue or sea green. Her hair is often decorated with red flowers.

In some stories, she was born human. As a girl, she was a skilled, fearless warrior. She had two brothers who were jealous of her natural flair for combat and knew she was far more capable than they were. When she excelled at these things, they were made to look weak and ineffective. They grew to hate her and, in time, resolved to kill her. Knowing she could easily defend herself, they attacked her when she was alone and asleep.

Despite being ambushed in this way, Iara fought back until her two brothers were left slain on the ground. Perhaps she was dreaming that she was in an epic fight.

Iara's father was full of rage when he saw his sons were dead. Without pausing to hear what had happened and mad with grief, he had Iara bound and thrown into the confluence of the rivers Negro and Solimões.

Turning his back on his daughter, he left her to drown.

The Tupi moon goddess, Jaci, had seen what had happened. She knew Iara was blameless. She elevated the girl's spirit and made her into the river goddess.

Here, her story becomes conflated with the European traditions of mermaids and sirens. She was no longer revered for her skills as a warrior. Her beauty and wonderful singing tend to define her. It is said men are driven insane by the sweetness of her voice.

In chronicles published by Portuguese colonists in the 16th century, there is mention of a horrible river monster called the Ipupiara. Its female form is a possible ringer for Iara, as she is described as very beautiful and has some elements of a human woman, including long, flowing hair.

The male Ipupiara is a different matter altogether. Pero de Magalhães Gândavo wrote in his 1564 account about a young indigenous woman who had been enslaved by the colonists. She was named Irecê. She had arranged to meet her lover on a São Vicente beach, only to find he had been brutally mauled by an Ipupiara monster. When she fled in horror and reported what had happened, a Portuguese captain found it and killed it with his sword.

This awful creature was described as being "fifteen hands" (3.3 meters) and "strewn with hair all over its body ... (and) on its snout it had very large silks like moustaches."

The Jesuit priest Fernão Cardim reported even more alarming details. He declared the Ipupiara was "repulsive" and said it killed humans by hugging them tightly and kissing them until they could no longer breathe, smothering them to death. It ate its victims, devouring their eyes, noses, fingertips, toes, and genitals. It was, Fernão Cardim said, "a bestial, hungry, disgusting being, of primitive and brutal ferocity." Historians generally assume that these early colonizers were waxing lyrical about some particularly aggressive form of sea lion or manatee.

Iara often appears in the story of Ruiva ("Red Beard") as a benevolent spirit for good. Long ago, in the state of Piauí in the northeastern region of Brazil, there was a young woman who found herself pregnant after her lover had died. She did not dare tell her family. When the time came for her baby to be born, she slipped away into the forest and gave birth to a son.

Afraid of what her mother and sisters would say, she put him in a copper pot and set him adrift in the river. As she left, a water spirit, often said to be Iara, resolved to save this baby boy, who came to be known as Ruiva. In the process of rescuing the baby, that area of the river became enchanted, which is how the Parnaguá lagoon came to be.

From then on, Ruiva would occasionally appear on the riverbank. In the morning, he seemed to be a baby, and passersby were alerted to his presence by his cries. However, by midday, he would be an amorous adult man with a red beard, desperate to steal a kiss from any young lady he might come across. By evening, he would be a wizened old man.

Another water spirit, Caboclo d'Água ("hillbilly from the waters"), is a creature that resembles a man who harasses fishermen and sailors on the São Francisco River. He forces boats to capsize, releases fish from nets, and even drowns unfortunates swimming in the river.

Caboclo d'Água is often described as a sort of merman with a copper-colored scaly fishtail. His hands are webbed like a frog's, and sometimes, he has a single eye in the center of his forehead.

Sailors and fishermen believed they could avoid his attention by painting a white star on the bottom of their boats or by decorating the bow with a carved carranca figurehead. A carranca could be a human or an animal, but it typically had a wide open mouth and fangs. It was thought the carranca would repel evil spirits from the water.

Some people prefer to try and curry favor with Caboclo d'Água by offering him tobacco or alcohol. If he accepts the gift, he might treat the giver with respect and even guide them toward waters with plenty of fish.

One of the most delightful creatures found only in the Amazon River is the pink dolphin known as the *boto* or *bufeo*. They are found in the basins of the Amazon and Orinoco across South America. It is the largest species of river dolphin; some males grow up to nine feet in length. They are born grey, and as they mature, they become glorious shades of pink, from a pale blush rose to a vibrant shade of bubblegum. Some remain grey with the merest hint of the famous pink, and some develop spots of pink that cover their bodies. It is still not certain why and how they develop in this way. It is possible that their diet, which is rich in shellfish, could play a role. Or perhaps it is a reaction to the sunlight or exposure to the sun. It seems their blood capillaries are nearer to the surface of their skins than in other dolphins, and this may make them appear pinker when aroused or threatened.

Despite their obvious similarities with sea dolphins, the boto has a very different psyche. It is just as agile, but it does not follow boats or jump out of the water. It generally manages to curb its natural curiosity in the presence of humankind. It lives in quiet, small family groups or with its mate and tends to prefer the calmer waters of the Amazon lagoons or flooded areas of the rainforest to stretches of the fast-flowing, open river.

The people who live alongside the Amazon have had a long and complicated relationship with the boto. Their strangeness and ethereal quality have given rise to stories and superstitions that they are protected by some mystical powers, and it is generally accepted that it is bad luck to kill a boto and even worse luck to eat its meat. Naturalists eager to see the rare Amazonian manatee were often advised to befriend a boto since they were considered the elusive creature's guardian.

Fishermen on the Amazon in areas frequented by botos view them with some suspicion. Although some believe they are friends that will lead them to waters full of fish, the botos are also known for luring humans out into dangerous waters, where they quickly find themselves lost. It is said that some even deliberately sink fishing boats so that the fishermen drown.

Some cultures believe the pink dolphin was originally a warrior who was so successful that the world spirits put him under an enchantment before he threatened the very nature of the world. The most well-known and enduring story is that of Boto Cor-de-Rosa, a shapeshifting pink dolphin that appears during summer feasts and celebrations as a sharply dressed stranger.

One version of this myth tells the story of a young woman named Rosita. She was a charming, happy girl who was beloved by all her family. She loved to help her mother with the household chores and often went to collect water from the nearby river.

One warm day, the river sparkled invitingly, and she could not resist taking a swim. As she glided through the cool water, she noticed a young man sitting on the riverbank close to where she had left her clothes. When she finished her swim, she spoke to him. He told her he was a fisherman, and Rosita couldn't help noticing how attractive he was. She arranged to meet him the following day, and after they had met a number of times, she fell in love and spent the night with him.

Rosita's parents began to worry about her. She was spending so much time at the river. When they confronted her, she told them all about her mysterious fisherman and said she wanted to marry him.

Trusting his beloved daughter's judgment, Rosita's father invited the fisherman to the family home and welcomed him with open arms as they arranged for the wedding. The young man was a charming guest, and the family soon grew to love him. However, they couldn't help but wonder why he left each morning without fail and was not seen again until he returned in the evening.

One night, the family had a celebration with a large meal and plenty to drink. Everyone slept well. As the family began to rise, they were alarmed by a shrill screaming coming from Rosita's room. Her father picked up his gun and ran to see what could have happened.

There, beside Rosita on her bed, lay a huge pink dolphin. It tried to wriggle free and head toward the door, but her father raised his gun and shot it dead.

The young fisherman never returned, and Rosita soon found she was expecting a baby. Months later, she died in childbirth. Her baby? It was a pink dolphin calf.

There are many stories of boto men as seductive, feckless lovers who leave young women pregnant and abandoned. In these accounts, the boto is universally dressed in a sharp white suit and, most importantly, a hat. This covers their blowholes, which would give away their true identities. Sometimes, the hat is a shapeshifted (or modified) stingray. Many of the boto man's accessories come from river creatures. For instance, he might wield an electric eel sword or wear catfish shoes. In its creature form, an enchanted boto with the ability to shapeshift can sometimes be spotted by its fin tips that look a little bit like human hands.

At odds with the solitary and quiet demeanor of the boto, once these entities have shapeshifted, they are the life and soul of the party. In one Amazon town, two men with hats enjoyed an evening of hard drinking and a great deal of raucous laughter. At dawn, they were seen leaving town, arm in arm, singing at the top of their voices and carrying bottles. The next day, fishermen caught two botos. While gutting them, the men were overcome by the stench of liquor that emanated from the dolphins' stomachs.

In another account, a sharp-dressed man, complete with a hat, was pestering young women with such persistence that the men of the village felt compelled to see him off. As their cries grew louder, a crowd joined in the chase. As he ran toward the river, three harpoon shots were fired at him. A dead boto washed up on shore shortly afterward with three harpoon darts embedded in its hide.

Some boto men are not quite the love 'em and leave 'em Lotharios. They prefer to lure young women to an underwater kingdom known as Encante. Once the young woman has entered its gates, she can never leave.

These myths were often used to explain unmarried women's pregnancies or pregnancies stemming from incest, prostitution, and rape. The white suit and accessories associated with the shapeshifting boto have some similarities to the white Europeans. Since the colonists violently subjugated the indigenous people, at times killing, raping, and traumatizing the women, it is possible that the boto has borne the brunt, in an allegorical fashion, of some of the most horrible experiences certain Amazon people groups suffered.

Chapter Four – Jaguar Tales

The jaguar, the third largest cat in the world, is native to South America, with half of its population in Brazil. These magnificent creatures are formidable hunters. They will prey on almost any animal they come across. Their strong jaws and sharp teeth can even penetrate hard crocodile skin or turtle shells.

Adult jaguars are solitary creatures that require large territories. They are confident swimmers and the epitome of power and grace. As a result, they have long been regarded with awe and respect by the people who live in the rainforest regions, and they have taken an integral role in Brazilian mythology.

Onça-Boi is the man-eating jaguar that is part of the oral traditions of Amazonas, especially Acre. He is closely connected with the spirit world, but in his earthly form, he can easily be distinguished from regular jaguars by his feet, which are hoofed. He is also said to have horns in some cultures.

Because he has no claws, he cannot climb trees and tends to go hunting with his mate. Then, one of them rests while the other eats, which is markedly different behavior from regular jaguars, which lead solitary lives outside of their breeding seasons. In the stories, people unfortunate enough to encounter the Onça-Boi often make the mistake of climbing a tree, believing they will be safe there. They do not realize that it will wait patiently until its prey is exhausted. When they inevitably fall asleep and tumble from the tree branches, the jaguar creature is waiting below.

The next day, Uaica couldn't wait to return to the tree and hear the whispering voice of Sinaa. Again, he found several sleeping animals and curled up with them. The jaguar man continued to tell him his secrets. Day after day, he slept under the tree without eating or running around like the other children. Soon, his grandfather could see that he was wasting away.

Sinaa also began to realize that the boy was sick. As Uaica slept under the tree, Sinaa whispered to him that he had shared his secrets and that he should leave and never come back again.

When Uaica woke, he felt sad. He knew he would miss the jaguar man, whom he had come to love as much as his grandfather, but he had promised that he wouldn't return, and he meant to keep his word.

When he arrived home, he found his grandfather weeping. The old man said it was breaking his heart to see Uaica so pale and frail and begged him to eat. Uaica sat down and shared a meal with him and then told him that he had a secret. After they had eaten, he took his grandfather to the dreaming tree in the forest.

Just as before, there were animals fast asleep around its trunk. As soon as Uaica began to feel drowsy, he told his grandfather that he could go no farther. The old man was curious and drew closer. It did not take too long for him to fall fast asleep between two snoozing peccaries. Uaica watched from a distance.

When Uaica's grandfather awoke, he told him never to tell anyone about the tree; its secrets were too powerful and dangerous for anyone who did not have a pure heart.

As they neared their village, the father of Casimiro, one of the boys who had teased Uaica mercilessly, was weeping. His son had become sick, and the family were preparing for him to die. Uaica asked to see Casimiro. He laid his hands upon the sick boy, and through the healing magic Sinaa had whispered to him, he was healed.

From then on, he and Casimiro became firm friends. There was no more teasing or cruel tricks. Uaica also helped to cure other people who fell sick in his village. He was wise beyond his years, and everyone grew to love and respect this strange young man.

One night, while Uaica was sleeping, the jaguar man visited him again. He told him to build a special house with his grandfather so Sinaa could share more of his secrets with him as he slept. Once the dreaming house had been built, Sinaa told Uaica more secrets about the forest and how to make beautiful things from items he could find there. Guided by his mentor, he collected feathers, flowers, stones, nuts, and shells and created intricate, beautiful jewelry and accessories that everybody wanted.

Although Uaica was happy to teach his creative skills to the other villagers, there was a woman who was particularly envious and resentful of his talent. She resolved to steal the loveliest pieces he had made. She had no idea, however, that Sinaa had taught him how to see everything. Uaica rounded on her. He told her and her friends that because of their greed, they no longer deserved his healing powers.

Then, he vanished, never to be seen again. No one knew what had become of him. Perhaps he was transported to a cave where he could spend the rest of his days dreaming, or maybe he became a spirit so he could join the jaguar man in that strange spirit world beyond the reach of humans.

Chapter Five – Monstrous Beasts

Brazilian folklore has more than its share of monsters, most of which are bloodthirsty maneaters, each with their own individual characteristics.

The Brazilian werewolf, the lobisomem, originates in the Amazon Basin region and is thought to be the product of an incestuous relationship or the offspring of a woman and an ordained priest.

Unlike the European werewolf, which has to wait for a full moon, the lobisomem changes from man to beast if it reaches a crossroads on a Friday night. During Lent, it can transform daily. Once the lobisomem has shed its human form, it rampages the countryside in search of children who have not been baptized. It devours these children with all the savagery of a wild beast.

Earlier accounts of the lobisomem suggest its bestial figure was not always wolfish. Rather, it was a dog, a wild pig, or a cross between the two. He has thick fur, glaring red eyes, and a pungent, rancid odor. Like the wolfman, he walks on his hind legs, but he can run more swiftly than most animals. In his human form, he is a weak individual, sometimes with pointed ears that give away his horrible other life.

The lobisomem can be killed with a thorn from a particular orange plant that has grown on consecrated ground or with a bullet that has been filled with wax from a candle that has been used for three holy Masses. If he is wounded, anyone who touches his blood will be doomed.

The Lobisomem do Acre was reported to have killed calves and a child in Seringal Sardinha in July 1990. Rubber tappers working there ran to the rescue after hearing something savaging the livestock. They said that they came face to face with a lobisomem.

The Gorjala, a monstrous, horrible ogre with one eye, lives on the rocky hills and cliffs of Ceará and Amazonas. He wears body armor made from turtle shells. He is huge and takes long strides that cause tremors. He hunts for humans, which he pops under an arm so he can eat them slowly as he trundles along.

The Labatut, another oversized, man-eating fiend, is best known in the Chapada do Apodi region. He also tends to have one eye like a Cyclops, but he also has thorns, spines, or thick stubby hairs that stick out of his body like a porcupine. He has tusks like a wild pig and runs through small communities at night looking for people to gobble up, preferably children because of their tender meat.

The Labatut is a relatively recent myth based on General Pedro (or Pierre) Labatut, who fought in the Brazilian War of Independence in the 19th century. He was a dreadful character. He was hated by his enemies and his own men for his excessive and needless brutality. Eventually, his army rose up against him. His abject cruelty has led to his reputation living on in Brazilian folklore.

In the northeastern reaches of Brazil, in the Alagoas region, the Pai do Mato is a ghastly giant that terrifies people at night with his maniacal, shrieking laughter that can be heard from miles away. Similar to the other ogres, he is huge, ugly, and hairy. He is supposed to be far taller than the trees in the forests where he dwells, and his footfalls make a booming sound. He can be distinguished (to a degree) by his claws or nails, which are long and sharp. Although he has a taste for human flesh, he tends to stay away from people, but if he is a threat, gunmen are encouraged to aim for his belly button, which is considered to be his weakest point.

The mapinguari, another monstrous creature, was supposed to inhabit the Amazon Rainforest. Its name derives from the Tupi-Guaraní words *mbappé*, *pi*, and *guari*, meaning "a being that has a crooked paw."

According to the story, an ancient shaman discovered the secrets of immortality, which angered the universe since it threatened to unbalance time and existence. Because of this, he was transformed into the horrible mapinguari as punishment and forced to remain in this form for all of eternity.

Descriptions vary, but these creatures are said to be covered in thick, dark, and shaggy fur, which is conveniently bulletproof. The indigenous people from the Tapajós River recount that it can be some three meters tall. Its skin is scaly, and like a caiman, it has large, sharp claws and sometimes just one eye.

Although comparable to a Cyclops, it has been suggested that this entity originated from some unidentified ape or giant ground sloth.

The mapinguari is focused on protecting its fragile environment and is supposed to stalk hunters who venture into the rainforest. When it captures them, it will twist their heads from their bodies before devouring them.

The Brazilian centaur, known as Besta-Fera ("Ferocious Beast"), is another mythical creature that arrived with the Portuguese settlers. He is widely accepted as a representation of the devil or one of his attendants. On the full moon, he may climb out of hell and into the mortal world from the graves of sinners in cemeteries. Once he has shaken himself free, he sets to work, marauding through the streets. When he comes across anyone, he brands them with his mark, and from then on, they are destined to burn in hell.

Some versions have Besta-Fera roaming the forests in search of some pernicious plant with a blood-red flower that is imbued with evil powers. Anyone who crosses his path will be rendered insane.

He is said to have the body of a horse and a human torso, arms, and head. He is accompanied by a pack of wild, snarling dogs, which he whips from time to time. With this same strap, he often metes out lashes to any other people or animals he comes across.

In the northeastern regions of Brazil, Besta-Fera is sometimes used as an insult to describe someone who has been unkind or aggressive.

Boi-Vaquim, a mythological creature from Rio Grande do Sul and the southern states of Brazil, is one of the creatures described by the celebrated poet and historian Contreira Rodrigues (1884–1960). It is a magnificent, mystical bull with golden horns, diamond eyes, and great wings. As it gallops, its horns create sparks of fire.

Unsurprisingly, it is incredibly difficult—perhaps impossible—to rope Boi-Vaquim. Cowboys have been driven mad by their obsession to match their skills against him. Some dread the possibility of an encounter with Boi-Vaquim.

In São Paulo, a different beast marauds the streets at nighttime: Porca dos Sete Leitões ("the Sow with Seven Piglets"). This pig is immense. She snorts and grunts with relish as she determinedly leads her brood that trot along in her wake. She was once, it is said, a baroness who had seven children. She was a proud, cruel woman. When she offended a spirit, she was transformed into her current porcine state. She can only become human again when she finds a magic ring.

In another version, she aborted seven pregnancies, and for doing that, she was made into a monster, with her unborn babies becoming piglets. In another version, the lost babies were due to her violent and cruel husband, and as Porca dos Sete Leitões, she is destined to harass errant husbands, persuading them to return to their families as better men.

In the city of Palmeira dos Índios in Algoas, sometime toward the very end of the 19th century, there lived a rich young woman who was the daughter of a powerful high-ranking officer in the military. She was an unpleasant person. She was self-obsessed and oblivious to the hardships and suffering of others.

This young woman had a pet dog that she adored. She spoiled him with endless treats, and he slept on the softest bed until he died on the same day as the spiritual leader of northeastern Brazil, a priest called Father Cicero. The young woman demanded that her beloved pet should have a full funeral Mass and a wake with a candle and sentinel to guard its soul. This funeral cost far more than most in the city could afford for their own family.

This young woman was at the market buying perfume and frivolous clothes a little while afterward when she came across an old woman who was bowed with grief. She was buying black clothes. The outspoken girl, knowing full well the effect of the loss of the priest upon the community, asked the old woman why she was mourning. When she heard it was for Father Cicero, the young woman laughed and said she would do better grieving for her little dog. However, as the words left her mouth, she snapped at the poor old woman. She fell on all fours and then bounded away like an animal.

By the time she had reached her home, it was hard to see where the woman ended and the dog began. She had cursed herself with her careless words, and her family was compelled to lock her away, fearing the shame she brought upon them. When her parents died, her brother, who felt little sympathy for her, had her locked in a cage, where she

The Onça da Mão Torta ("Crooked Hand Jaguar") is a mythical beast that stalks the savanna of Goiás. It has different markings than the big cats native to South America and is striped like a tiger. One of its front paws is twisted and buckled, but this doesn't seem to hinder it from hunting and performing other activities.

He is said to be resistant to gunfire and is the spirit of a nomadic cowboy, much like the myth from the Minas Gerais region of Brazil of a shabby, mysterious cowboy who seems to possess mysterious powers. He is neither young nor old, has a slight build, is relaxed in his demeanor, and rarely speaks. His old horse is thin and as decrepit in appearance as he is. He will unexpectedly appear when there are competitions on farms and ranches, such as ox felling, ring racing, and other races. The other cowboys always defer to his skills and knowledge and are always pleased to see the small figure in his large leather floppy hat that hides his oversized forehead and long beard.

One day, a wealthy farmer in Urucuia was having difficulties rounding up his horses, which were spread out over a huge area. He had the idea of organizing a competition that would be open to anyone who thought they could find his horses and drive them back. He would hold, as was traditional, a great feast for all those intending to compete.

Cowboys and ranchers came from all over arrived. They met at the farm and greeted each other warmly, all eager to prove their worth against each other. But before they could saddle up, a mysterious cowboy was bringing the farmer's horses home. He refused to take any prize or reward and slipped away unnoticed as the party was underway.

The cowboys and herdsmen were not at all surprised, but they could not understand how he managed to do it. Whenever they saw him, he was ambling along on a tired old horse.

Sometime later, farmers began finding their cattle were suffering violent attacks. Something was leaving them dead or gored and torn with horrific injuries. The cowboys gathered to find the cause and try to prevent more valuable cattle from being affected. As they discussed what kind of beast they were dealing with, they realized the mysterious cowboy was not there. They speculated that perhaps he had died or was badly wounded. Perhaps he simply could not be bothered to help. As they spoke, their respect for him gave way to ill will and jealousy.

The next day, they started setting out when the familiar small, shabby figure appeared over the horizon with a herd of wild bulls, the very beasts that had terrorized the cattle. The farmer was delighted, but the gathered men were uneasy and couldn't see how he could have achieved such a feat on his own. They began to suspect he was using witchcraft.

One of the younger cowboys resolved to find out the strange man's secrets and befriended him. The two men rode across the land, rarely speaking, even at the campfires where they cooked simple meals before they slept under the stars.

After the months passed, there was little food available, and the mysterious cowboy's companion began to grow weak from lack of nourishment. One morning, when he struggled to mount his horse, the other man handed him some leaves and told him to wait. He explained that he was going to transform himself into a jaguar to hunt for something they could eat, and as soon as he returned, the young man should stuff the leaves into his mouth. Then, he would return to his human state.

The young man watched him go and wondered whether he had heard correctly in his weakened state. To his surprise, in the bright morning sun, the slight figure of the cowboy seemed to become dappled, and it leaped with all the power and grace of a large cat.

It was not long before a large jaguar returned, snarling, with the hindquarters of some beast in its jaws. It dropped the meat and turned to the young cowboy, but he was terrified. Despite his weakened state, he managed to get on his horse and ride away. He still had the leaves in his hands when he finally came to rest.

As for the mysterious cowboy, he remained a jaguar, roaming the state in search of the young man who knows his secret and can help him become human again.

In other stories, the mysterious cowboy is a shapeshifter who is able to take the form of a jaguar, and some of the problems he was so eager to help with were actually caused by him while in his jaguar state. As he spent more and more time as a big cat, he grew more feline than human. When the ranchers realized that it was him attacking livestock on their farms, hunters in the region resolved to put an end to him. Eventually, they managed to corner him and shot him dead.

In one rather more sentimental version of this story, his young cowboy companion was among the hunters who corned him. As the trapped jaguar saw his traitorous friend amongst his captors, he gave one last moan of sadness—an unmistakably human sound of misery and remained until the end of her days.

The headless mule is a common theme in Brazilian mythology. The most commonly held belief is that its origins are from medieval Europe, probably Iberia, and the story came to Brazil with the Portuguese colonists in the 16th century.

This Mula Sem Cabeça is generally considered to have been a woman who has been cursed for her sins. The mule varies in its appearance from state to state, but it is generally brown or black with silver or iron hooves that clatter and make an alarming noise. Smoke and flames sometimes billow from its neck where its head should be. Despite having no mouth (although some suggest she does have a head but that it is obscured by fire), it makes a shrill neighing sound or wails and cries like a human woman.

The poor woman who became the Mula Sem Cabeça was either a girl who had sexual relations before her marriage or a woman who entered into a relationship with a priest. For this, she is cursed to gallop over seven parishes, starting and finishing where she committed her sinful act. In some versions of the story, the enchantment ends each morning with the crowing of the rooster. She then returns to her human state, exhausted and naked except for her bridle. At nightfall, she will become a mule and gallop again.

In other versions, she tears through fields and forests, devouring any unfortunate creature in her path. There are several ways to stop her, such as pulling her tack from her, which is no mean feat since it is often said to be red-hot. If it is removed, the curse can be resumed if she is re-bridled.

Failing that, drawing her blood with a needle might stop her, which is somewhat easier than tying her to a cross, which is another cure. Once free of the curse, naked (again), grateful, and faintly smelling of sulfur, she will repent her sins. Tellingly, the priest who broke his vows by entering into this relationship did not suffer any known curses or indignities; the responsibility appears to lay exclusively at his lover's feet.

An unusual mythical being that is said to roam the states of Piauí, Minas Gerais, Mato Grosso, and Rondônia is the pé de garrafa ("Bottle Foot"). He has one leg, and because of this, he is supposed to leave tracks behind him that look like a bottle has been dragged along the ground, similar to footprints left by the giant sloth, which is thought to explain the origin of this entity.

The pé de garrafa is part man with a horn in the center of its forehead. It is covered in hair. It can imitate human voices and lure people deep into the forests, where they quickly become lost. It is not as bloodthirsty as some of the other Brazilian mythological creatures, but it will send people mad with its strange and stupefying gaze.

In the Minas Gerais region, especially in São Paulo, people tell the myth of Corpo Seco ("Dry Body"), a man who was so evil and cruel during his long life that when he died, both the angels and the devil refused to take him. His family buried him, but even the earth refused to accept his body. It laid in its grave, entire and uneaten by worms, never decomposing.

Some claim he was from Monteiro Lobato in Serra da Mantiqueira. He held his parents in a dark cellar and beat them for no reason. He subjected everyone he met to spite and hatred and was killed by a vigilante. The people of Monteiro Lobato loathed him so much that they spat on his grave.

After a long time, he rose from his grave. In the long years that had passed, his hair and nails had grown long, and his body was spindly and emaciated. He crept around at nighttime, hiding and occasionally wailing in self-pity at his predicament. He is sort of like a zombie. He is as evil in death as he is in life, and he kills anyone he comes across by crushing their bodies with his thin, dry arms.

In the state of Piauí in northeastern Brazil, the Cabeça de Cuia ("Gourd Head") is the bizarre specter that protects the rivers Parnaíba and Poty.

The story starts with a young man, Crispim, who lived by the banks of the Parnaíba River with his family. They were poor and relied on the river for food, but it was a hard life. There were periods when there was little fish to be caught, especially during the flood season.

One day, Crispim took the boat out, hoping to catch something for lunch, but there was nothing. Dejected and hungry, he returned home, cursing his bad fortune and his family's lack of funds and food.

His mother, seeing him so despondent, felt sorry for him and went to her neighbor to see if they could offer her something with which to make a meal. All the neighbor had was an ox bone, which they handed to her.

Crispim's mother did her best, but with nothing else available other than a little flour, she could do nothing but boil the bone to make a thin broth. When her son sat down to eat, having spent so many hours fruitlessly trying to fish, he was appalled to be served this bone water. In anger, he seized the bone and threw it at his unfortunate mother, killing her. Crispim did not even try to help her. Instead, he ran away as fast as he could.

As she lay dying, the poor woman cursed her son, and as Crispim ran, his head began to swell and grow until it resembled a large gourd.

No longer human, Cabeça de Cuia (which is what Crispim became) was left to wander Teresina, where the two rivers meet. He desperately wants to atone for his wicked deed and break his enchantment, but to do this, he must devour seven young virgins named Maria, which was the name of his mother.

Driven mad by the curse and in his search for Marias, he frequently and clumsily causes the deaths of bathers and those fishing in the rivers. With his horrible bloated head, he can breathe underwater and swim like a fish. He drags the people he kills to the depths of the rivers.

In a less bloodthirsty version of the myth, rather than being forced to murder and eat seven Marias, he is simply looking for his mother to beg for her forgiveness.

The Capelobo is a mythical beast particularly well known in the Maranhão, Amazonas, and Pará states. It is thought to originate with the indigenous people in those areas. Its name is from the indigenous Brazilian word *cape*, meaning "broken bone," and the Portuguese word *lobo*, which means "wolf," although its etymology is rather more complicated.

The Capelobo is part man but has hooves rather than feet, thick brown hair that entirely covers its body, and the head of a giant anteater. In some stories, its back legs are like those of a goat, and there is also the suggestion that it has some features of a tapir.

Although it generally has the head and mouth of a giant anteater, its diet does not consist of insects. It devours cats, dogs, and sometimes people, squeezing their bodies until they die and then drinking their blood. It also might pierce their skulls to feed on the brains with its long tongue.

The Capelobo lives in the rainforests and roams the wetter regions late at night, hoping to find plump kittens or puppies to feast on. It can be killed but only by a single rifle shot that pierces its belly button, which is a vulnerable part of the body of the more horrible characters in Brazilian mythology.

A common theme in Brazilian mythology is the concept of mystic, floating body parts. A good example of this is the Cabeça Satânica ("Satanic Head"), a bizarre being as vile as its name suggests. It almost certainly originates from Portuguese folklore, with its roots firmly in Christian hellfire and damnation and designed to keep medieval Europeans in line. It is thought to have gained a foothold in Brazilian lore from colonizers who arrived in the Pernambuco region, but its influence spread throughout the country. It is still feared in some of the more remote areas of Brazil.

Cabeça Satânica is exactly as its name suggests: the disembodied head of a devil that somehow suspends itself in the air late at night. Some of those who recount seeing it explain that it rolls or bounces along the ground before finding an appropriate place to drift in the air. Others say it is carried or led by some kind of specter that melts away when the horrible head finds its prey.

It is usually described as red, sometimes glowing, with a manic grin and, more often than not, long straggling hair (by which its ghost carries it). Its eyes are deathly and unforgettable, and its other features are crude and ugly. It spits fire and has a shrill, cackling laugh.

Of course, as you may expect, it has evil intent. Anyone who touches it or is unlucky enough to have it fall onto them will quickly fall sick and die in a matter of days. In some stories, it can devour people whole. It seems to have no origin story. No one knows who it was or where it came from, and its victims appear to be chosen at random. Those who are unfortunate enough to have an encounter with it are advised to make the sign of the cross or, if they have a straw Palm Sunday cross available, to throw it at him and then quickly run away. These same crosses can be pinned to doors to keep it at bay.

In the state of Pará, there is another floating head, the Cumacanga (or Curacanga), to fear. This head was originally a woman who had an affair with a priest. In other stories, it is the head of the seventh consecutive daughter born in a family. To prevent this fate from befalling a seventh daughter, it became traditional for the sixth daughter to become the baby's godmother.

This head has fiery hair and floats from its body at night, scaring people in the dead of night before returning to its body at the first morning crow of the rooster. If someone sees the disembodied head and offers her a needle, the next day, the (entire) woman is compelled to betrayal—before the bullet was fired. It is said that those who were there could never forget it.

Another jaguar myth from the state of Minas Gerais that is particularly prevalent amongst the Xakriabá people, is Kianumaka-Maña. There are several similarities with the mysterious cowboy myth, but Kianumaka-Maña is no humble cowboy; she is a goddess.

Kianumaka-Maña is a warrior. She is able to harness the strength and cunning of the jaguar. The indigenous people who revered her performed rituals before going into battle in the hope of imbuing her ferocity and fighting skills. She also represents freedom and self-sufficiency and is sometimes depicted as a beautiful woman painted with the markings of the jaguar.

As well as obvious comparisons with the mysterious cowboy, Kianumaka-Maña is a goddess in the tradition of the Greek Artemis and the Roman Diana (goddesses of hunting), the ancient Egyptian lion goddess Sekhmet, and the Norse giantess goddess Skadi that rules over winter and hunting.

In one story, a mother and daughter were out when the mother complained they had little meat to eat recently. The daughter told her she would kill a cow for them, but when she came back, she told her mother to push a branch into her mouth.

The daughter left. Soon afterward, the mother heard the sound of a heifer being attacked by a jaguar. Suddenly, the jaguar leaped toward the mother with its jaws wide open, ready for her to throw the branch between its teeth. However, the mother fled in terror.

The girl never became human again. In the daytime, she hid, and at night, she attacked the farmers' cattle until they begged her to stop, handing her their branding irons as a mark of good faith.

In a related story, a girl named Yndaiá felt bitter and angry about the colonization and invasion of her homeland. In a bid to avenge herself on the cruel Europeans who had settled in the region, she asked a shaman to invoke the spirit of the jaguar and enchant her with it.

Once she was able to shapeshift into the form of a jaguar, she attacked the cattle of these farmers and dragged the meat back to her village, where it could be shared. Whenever she returned, Yndaiá's mother (a much braver woman in this story) would be waiting with a branch to throw into the jaguar's mouth so she could transform into a girl again.

However, one day, the mother was unable to find the particular type of branch required to break the enchantment, so Yndaiá could not shapeshift back into her human form. The worst was to come. The farmers got a posse together to hunt the big cat that had been targeting their livelihoods.

Jaguar-Yndaiá, now the hunted, managed to make her way to a cave and remained there, wondering if her end was near. However, her people had not forgotten her and her generosity and brought her meat. They quietly made their way to the cave and performed rituals and dances all through the night until she became a girl again.

The dreaming tree is another myth with the jaguar at its heart. A young boy, Uaica, lived with his elderly grandfather in a small village. He was not a strong child. The other children were often cruel and made fun of him when he could not join in their games.

One day, these teasing remarks were too much for Uaica. He didn't want to go back to his grandfather, knowing the old man would worry since he loved him so much. Instead, he walked into the forest. He had a great love for nature, and the lush green plants and cool air, perfumed with exotic blooms, made him feel calmer and happier.

Uaica was about to turn back when he stumbled. After climbing to his feet, he saw the most extraordinary sight. Beneath a large tree was a tapir lying alongside a sloth, fast asleep. As he drew closer, as quietly as he dared, he saw there was also an anaconda, a monkey, a caiman, and a mother jaguar with her cubs, all sleeping soundly curled up beside each other.

Uaica suddenly felt weary. He was unable to keep his eyes open, and he joined the animals beneath the tree. As he slept, he dreamed he could hear Sinaa's voice.

Uaica had heard stories of Sinaa since he could remember. He was the magical jaguar man with eyes in the back of his head, and he appeared to be an old man until he bathed. Then, his old skin fell away, and he became a young and handsome man. Sinaa knew all of the secrets of the world, such as where the great forked stick that held up the sky could be found, how to save the world from the perils it faced, and how to heal sick animals and humans.

Sinaa whispered stories to the sleeping boy. Eventually, Uaica awoke. It was dark, and all the sleeping animals had gone.

return it, revealing the identity of the Cumacanga.

The Perna Cabeluda ("Hairy Leg"), another mythical body part with a mind of its own, is a leg covered in thick, dark fur that bounces or hops along the streets in the dead of night when everyone is sleeping. If it comes across a drunkard or an adulterer, it will trip them or give them a sharp kick.

This story began as a joke in the 1970s when a caller to a Recife radio show claimed he had found the leg in his bed, and his wife told him it was an autonomous being that had gotten there by itself. This story seemed to capture the public's imagination, and before long, it became an integral part of Brazilian folklore.

Some claim it was the limb of a wicked man who kicked his mother to death, and others say it was part of a dismembered body that the devil hurled from hell. There is also a rumor that it now has eyes and a mouth on its knee, which suggests the story may continue to develop as the years go by.

Chapter Six – Serpents, Snakes, and Worms

In southern Brazil, a mythical amphibious serpent or worm known as the Minhocão is believed to live or once lived deep beneath the ground and under the water. Described as a huge monster with hard black scales and possibly horns, its body is said to be approximately 20 to 50 meters in length (65 to 165 feet) but could be as long as 80 meters (260 feet). It causes earth tremors and landslides as it burrows underground.

The Minhocão de Parí that marauds the Cuiabá River in the state of Mato Grosso is a well-known example. It was said to attack and eat fishermen on that river when the fish were spawning. At other times, it wallowed in the mud, creating large swampy areas and damaging roads. It even dragged cattle and horses into its lair.

Unlike many of the mythological and legendary creatures of Brazil, there are several documented sightings of the Minhocão and some speculation as to its origins. In the state of Paraná, a young man saw a pine tree suddenly fall to the ground. When he hurried over to investigate, he realized the earth was moving below him, and he caught a glimpse of a massive worm-like creature with two horns driving through the mud. In that same state, a woman walking to a nearby pool for water found the area wrecked and an animal the size of a house crawling away. Some other people arrived too late to see the beast, but they did see the trail its body had left behind.

shifted so that the canoe was forced over the waterfalls. In some stories, the couple is falling for eternity.

In other stories, Naipi was turned into a distinctive central stone for her disobedience and disrespect of the river god. She is destined to be struck by the falling waters forever more. Tarobá became a palm tree on the edge of a cliff where he must watch his lover's torment. He stays there, powerless to help his love. Both are watched over by the vengeful M'Boi from his underwater lair, a cave known as Garganta do Diabo ("Devil's Throat"). Every so often, rainbows form the stretch from Naipi's stone to Tarobá's tree, a manifestation of their love, something that even M'Boi could not destroy.

Boitatá is a fabled land-dwelling snakelike beast that often has similar hypnotic powers to the boiúna. It is rather more ethereal, though, and is often described as a kind of fire snake composed entirely from colorful flames. Sometimes, it can appear as a ball of fire that floats, flies, or suspends itself in the air. It is possible that this myth is strongly influenced by the will-o-the-wisp phenomenon, the pale flames that are naturally produced above marshlands in the evenings.

The snakier version of this entity can breathe fire and is sometimes described as having two horns. It can disguise itself as a burning tree branch and has glowing eyes that blind or unbalance the minds of those who look into them, or it can mesmerize them sufficiently enough to eat their eyes. Anyone unfortunate enough to see the boitatá is warned to remain as still as possible with their eyes closed and to pray for it to pass by quickly.

Paradoxically, this fire snake's purpose is to protect the land from poachers who would set the forests alight. It is meant to frighten loggers who are intent on cutting down trees.

The version of the myth told in Rio Grande do Sul explains how the jungle emerged from the primordial darkness when floods began. Most of the animals ventured onto the higher lands. The Boiguaçu, a snake that lived in a cave, was the only creature able to see in the darkness. It preyed on the animals and ate their eyes until its own glowed and gleamed like two small suns. Its body grew to a great length and then began to burn. The Boiguaçu's body perished as it burned away. All the light from the eyes streamed out of them and created the sun. The boitatá was born at the same time, flying in the jungle skies in a swirl of flames.

In some northeastern regions of Brazil, the boitatá is a catch-all for all of the evil souls that have lived and then died. In the south, the myth has become entangled with the biblical story of Noah and the ark. Here, the snakes that survived the Great Flood, which was said to have freed the earth of wickedness, were punished by fire. Each was filled with flames.

Serpentes de Igreja, "church serpents," are another phenomenon in Brazilian mythology. This is the notion that immense snakes have been sleeping underground for centuries. They must remain undisturbed, or else the religious buildings directly over their heads or the tips of their tails will be destroyed. Sometimes, the entire city will be reduced to rubble.

There are a number of local rituals or processions necessary to keep the snakes sleeping, and these are still performed in São Luis in Maranhão, Lages in Santa Catarina, Itacotiara in Amazonas, Araraquara (this particular serpent is said to be an enchanted child) and Taubaté in São Paulo, and Belém and Óbidos in Pará. In time, however, these efforts will be futile since the snake will awaken when it grows so large that its tail enters its mouth.

The rural area of Santarém at the lower reaches of the Amazon in the state of Pará, northern Brazil, is home to the story of Cobra Honorato (or Norato) and Maria Caninana. The legend takes place in a village near the shores of a river where a young woman found she was expecting a baby. She had not had any sexual relations, but she had bathed in the river. In some versions of the story, she is attacked by the boiúna. When her time came, she gave birth to two black snakes.

Before they could slither away, her old Tapuya midwife baptized them Honorato and Maria. The two women allowed them to go back to the water from where they were descended. The two snakes grew to maturity in the river. The male snake, Cobra Honorato, was good and thoughtful. His half-human parentage enabled him to leave the river at nightfall on occasion and transform into a very handsome young man dressed all in white. On these evenings, he quietly made his way to the home of the old Tapuya woman, his godmother, and ate with her. He treated her with much respect and often stayed with her until it was time for him to slip back into his immense snakeskin and glide back into the waters. His godmother loved him very much.

Cobra Honorato was also sure to help the villagers whenever he could. He fought against predators that might decimate the fish they

An engineer named Émile Odebrecht once made a survey of the Santa Catarina uplands. He recorded several deep, irregular, and unexplained trenches that ran alongside a tributary. These were thought to have been caused by the movement of the Minhocão.

In 1849, a description of a dead Minhocão emerged. This account stated the creature's skin was as thick as the bark of a pine tree and had scales like an armadillo. The respected German biologist Fritz Müller theorized that perhaps the Minhocão could be some kind of giant armadillo thought to have been extinct. He also suggested it might be an oversized South American lungfish since it was said to be at its most active during prolonged periods of rain.

The Minhocão is not the only monstrous water snake in Brazilian mythology. The boiúna ("Giant Snake") is a malevolent presence that lurks in the darker corners of the rivers, lakes, and lagoons. This boiúna is a snake so colossally large that the grooves caused by its great undulating body in the shallows are said to have formed the rivers that flow from the Amazon. This snake makes an ominous rumbling sound and has large glowing eyes. Some of the indigenous Amazon people groups believe that it is not a lone spirit; rather, it is the creature that develops from a boa constrictor that continues to grow beyond the approximate eighteen feet (six meters), its maximum length.

The boiúna's shapeshifting ability is not confined to human or animal forms. It is able to assume the shape of a ghostly ship or steamer. When it takes this shape, it cruelly gives hope of rescue to those in peril on the water. With their own canoes capsized or sinking, they swim toward the strange craft promising salvation, little realizing they are hurrying toward their doom.

It also makes direct attacks on humans it encounters on the waters it regards as its territory and drags them down to the depths. There, it gorges upon them in the underwater caves it has dug itself. In a more fanciful story, it takes them to an underwater kingdom for the dead and transforms them into river snakes.

As it swims, the boiúna leaves a telltale V-shaped trail across the water's surface. It is often considered a protector of water life, but its presence in the water is sufficient enough to impregnate women bathing or swimming in those waters.

There is a more sinister and supernatural side to the boiúna. Its luminous eyes give it the ability to mesmerize its victims. It can then steal their shadows, leaving them to die as an *assombrado* ("one without a shadow"), a horrible and miserable demise, as the victim wastes away after a few days.

In the Tocantins River, there was a boiúna called Norato who frequently left the water and disguised himself as a handsome young man. He would dance and party with humans, leaving his snakeskin at the riverbank so it would be ready for his return. This worked well for some time until he carelessly forgot to conceal his skin in his eagerness to dance. A passerby found it. Supposing it might belong to a boiúna, they burned it. Norato returned to the water's edge after a night of high living, but he was unable to find his skin and forced to remain a human.

Unlike some of the monsters in Brazilian myths, the boiúna is considered intelligent. When it has been called upon during a séance, it can divulge a great deal about the underworld, at least according to spiritualists.

Its hypnotic powers can also affect ships, leaving them static and unable to move in remote waters. Many a sailor through the ages have wondered whether mechanical difficulties with their craft may be due to the powers of the boiúna.

The boiúna can be killed or disenchanted. After luring it to the riverbank with a bowl of fresh milk, its throat must be cut swiftly and cleanly, and then its killer must depart quickly without turning back.

The stunningly beautiful Iguazu ("Great Water") Falls are situated on the border between Brazil and Argentina. These are the falls Eleanor Roosevelt famously called "Poor Niagara" when she visited. This waterfall has been sacred to the indigenous Tupi-Guaraní people who lived in the vicinity since ancient times. Some worshiped the snake god M'Boi, who demanded human sacrifices from time to time.

A long time ago, there was a girl named Naipi, a chief's daughter, who was very lovely. Her beauty was such that rivers stopped flowing when she looked at her reflection in their waters. M'Boi demanded that she should be given to him. However, Naipi had already fallen in love with Tarobá, a dashing young man from a neighboring tribe. He had no intention of letting M'Boi have his beloved and arranged to rescue her in his canoe.

The night before the sacrificial ceremony, Naipi fled. They paddled along the river, but M'Boi quickly discovered what had happened. Furious, he began to shift his immense coils. As he moved, the land depended on and, on one occasion, spent three days fighting against catfish in the Trombetas River that had started stealing fish from the Claro River. He saved several people from drowning in the river and rescued damaged boats and canoes.

His sister, Maria Caninana, did not share her brother's personality. She was vicious and aggressive. She liked nothing more than making life unpleasant for the people her brother liked to help. She never visited her godmother. Instead, she preferred to attack solitary figures hunting for shellfish at the waterside and finding sailors clinging onto the wreckage of their boats after being hit by a storm and dragging them down to the bottom of the river.

In the river port of Óbidos in the state of Pará, there is a colossal serpent coiled beneath the municipality, fast asleep. Its head is supposedly beneath the altar dedicated to Santa Anna at Notre Dame, while the end of its tail lays at the bottom of the river. Everyone is aware that should it awaken, the church would collapse, and disaster would befall the people in that region.

Maria Caninana carefully combed the riverbed, searching for the end of the serpent's tail. When she finally found the tail, she bit it hard, hoping to wreak devastation. The serpent stirred, causing a tremor throughout the port, but it did not awaken.

Cobra Norato realized his sister would never stop her campaign to wreak misery on her mother's people, so with a heavy heart, he killed her. After spending some time alone to come to terms with what he had done, Cobra Norato went back to the village. He left his snake skin at the waterside, as he did when he visited his godmother, and found the people were sharing a meal. When they saw him dressed all in white, they made him welcome and asked him to eat with them.

Cobra Norato danced with the girls and chatted with the men. He was respectful to the elderly, and everyone was charmed by this polite, well-mannered young man. When the party came to an end, he disappeared. Just as his new friends realized he had left, they heard the sound of a great snake plunging into the river.

Cobra Norato became a regular visitor to the village. Every year, he pleaded for someone to break the curse so he might remain a handsome young man. He told them that if he was found in his snake form asleep on the riverbank with his mouth wide open, it would take three drops of mother's milk on his tongue and a cut to his head with a blade that had not been used before. His great jaws would snap shut, and after three drops of blood seeped from his head wound, he would walk away from his reptilian remains to enjoy a mortal life. His cast-off skin should then be burned so that no one else might suffer the same terrible enchantment.

Although the villagers felt a great deal of sympathy for Cobra Norato, there were few brave enough to approach him as he slept. His huge, sharp fangs were terrifying to behold. His close friends all carried vials of mother's milk and new blades with them, hoping to help, but they could not force themselves to approach him for the ritual he so craved.

Dejected, Cobra Norato took to swimming farther and farther away from the village, always hoping to meet someone prepared to help him. Eventually, he arrived at the town of Cametá. There, he shed his skin and mixed with the local people. He told them of his plight. A soldier heard him and was determined to help the poor young man.

He took a jar of mother's milk and found Cobra Norato sleeping on the riverbank with his mouth wide open, just as he had said. With no thought for his own safety, the soldier did as the young man had asked. As the blood oozed from his head, the curse was lifted, and Cobra Norato was finally able to start a new life as a human.

Chapter Seven – Brazilian Bogeymen

Brazilian children have been encouraged to behave out of fear of a variety of vile entities, much like the bogeyman. Most of these entities are thought to have been influenced by African traditions, with their stories told by the Black enslaved people brought to South America by the Portuguese colonists. These stories, however, have transformed as they passed through the generations.

Tutu Marambá is one of these horrible creatures. It eats children, and its area of interest is in those kids who won't go to sleep. It is usually described as a formless void of nothingness that hides behind the doors of children's rooms, although some stories say he is an immensely strong and hairy ogre that smells and sounds like a peccary. Another version, prevalent in the state of Bahia that binds these two ideas, sees Tutu Marambá as a shadow creature that is able to transform itself into a wild pig to utilize that creature's speed and strength.

The only known way to protect children from the attention of Tutu Marambá is with songs and lullabies, which are sung softly to an infant at bedtime.

"Bicho Tutu, sai de cima do telhado

Deixa esse menino dormir sossegado!"

"Tutu, get off the roof

Let this boy sleep peacefully!"

However, in the southern regions of Brazil, Tutu Marambá was an ancient warrior. He was a skilled spearman who never failed to fell his target, be it man or beast, and he diligently defended and protected the people of his village. His fame spread with his courageous deeds, and his people enjoyed living in security and treated their champion with gratitude and respect.

But this peace was shattered when an army of foreigners launched an attack. Tutu Marambá was killed by a poisoned dart as he battled to save his village. Sorrowfully, the people mourned him and carried his body to a sacred place where he would be remembered forever. As he was laid to rest, his soul soared away as a beautiful white bird, and this species has come to represent courage and bravery. There is no clear reason why the ancient warrior became a hideous bogeyman, but it is probably due to confusion brought about by their similar names.

The African enslaved people introduced or took on Tutu Marambá as a part of their culture in Brazil. The songs and stories they shared with their children were passed on to their children, and so on. Its name probably derives from the Kimbundu word for "ogre." This language was spoken by those from the Angola region of the African continent.

The indigenous people in the northern regions call this entity Tutu Zambê, a monster with twisted, crooked legs—often crippled—and sometimes headless. This one does not have the patience of the Tutu Marambá. Rather than waiting at doors, it prefers to wander the forests in search of young or vulnerable victims.

Children who cry in the Minas Gerais state of Brazil are at risk of being eaten by the Chibamba, a half-human, half-beast that covers itself with banana leaves. It constantly moves as if it were dancing and is thought to originate from old African stories brought to Brazil by enslaved workers on Portuguese plantations.

Cabra Cabriola is another creature that children feared, but this entity originated from Portuguese folklore. It is a hideous nanny goat with flaming eyes and nostrils that eats naughty boys and girls. It can get into houses by opening doors or climbing in from the rooftops. It is said that when little children cry in their sleep, it is because Cabra Cabriola has taken another victim to feast upon.

Its feet clatter as it runs across the rooftops, and it sings this somewhat manic little song to that rhythm:

"Eu sou a Cabra Cabriola
Que como meninos aos pares
Também comerei a vós
Uns carochinhos de nada!"
"I am Cabra Cabriola
Who eats children in pairs,
And I will eat you too,
A few little oldies!"

Parents in the northwestern states of Sergipe, Bahia, and Alagoas who fear their children are at risk from this monstrous goat advise them to get on their knees and pray. This is their only hope when it approaches their homes.

There is a Brazilian lullaby sung to babies and little ones with an ominous warning:

"Nana neném que a Cuca vem pegar
Papai foi para a roça, mamãe foi trabalhar."
"Baby, that Cuca is coming to get you,
Daddy has gone to the farm, and Mummy has gone to work."

Cuca is a witch in the European tradition that has found its place in Brazilian folklore. She is a horrible, wizened hag set on abducting and harming children. The first Cuca hatched from an egg at the beginning of time, and after a thousand years, she became a songbird renowned for her mournful song. After that, a newly hatched Cuca takes her place.

Unlike her European witchy cousins, Cuca is a spirit that invades the dreams and subconscious, frightening her victims with the most terrifying nightmares. She only sleeps one night every seven years.

Yet another threat to children, this time in the Recife region, is the Palhaço do Coqueiro ("the Clown in the Coconut Tree"), a horrible clown who steals children in order to sell their organs. This is a recent corruption of a mythical clown who was so unsuccessful in his efforts to entertain circus audiences that he ran away. Driven insane by his failure, he climbs into coconut palms to see the moon, which seems to be smiling down at him.

When the moon wanes or on cloudy nights, he climbs down and tries to amuse the people he comes across. If they don't laugh, he flies at them in a rage and often kills them.

Papa-Figo ("Liver Eater") also seeks a supply of children to dismember. He is an elderly man with a long nose and sharp teeth and claws. He carries a large sack on his back in which he puts the bodies of children who tell lies. If he cannot get hold of suitable children, he will take freshly dead bodies from cemeteries.

He is supposed to suffer from some disease, probably the potentially fatal tropical parasitic chagas disease that broke out in the northeast of Brazil. He believes eating the livers of children will help cure him. The usual treatment for those suffering from chagas was a liver puncture.

In the state of Bahia, there is another bogeyman entity, the Quibungo. This truly awful creature, believed to be of the Angola and Congo tradition, is a hybrid of creatures, including an ape, a vicious dog, and sometimes a wild pig. It is distinguishable from other fantastic Brazilian beasts by the second huge mouth on its back, which it uses to devour children whole.

In one commonly held tale, the horrible Quibungo finds a little girl playing outside on her own one evening. He grabbed her in his second mouth and then made off, intending to enjoy eating her at his leisure back in his cave.

The little girl started to sing from inside the Quibungo's mouth, asking her mother to come and save her. Her mother, however, had warned her not to play outside on her own in the dark. Though she heard the sad little song, she refused to help.

The little girl continued to sing, but her other relatives took the same stance as her mother, and no one made any effort to save her until the Quibungo approached the house where the girl's grandmother lived. This old woman quickly filled a pot with boiling water. As he passed, confident that he wouldn't be challenged for his supper, she threw the water over his feet, scalding him.

As the Quibungo fell to his knees in agony, his back mouth opened to howl in pain, and the little girl hopped out. Her grandmother hadn't finished with the child-eating fiend. She stabbed him in the neck with a burning skewer, killing him.

The little girl remained with her grandmother and never played out at night again, as there were plenty more Quibungos willing to snatch a tasty young child.

Cautionary tales are not restricted to bogeymen characters. There are also witch-type characters that are influenced by the European tradition;

these figures likely have their origins in the Portuguese culture that developed in Brazil.

In folklore from the northern regions of Brazil, Matinta Pereira was an old woman with the ability to shapeshift into a bird. In her earliest form, it was said that she could communicate with animals in their own languages and that she had the ability to control the weather and even summon storms. Her story has since developed. Rather than being the wise woman of the forest with musical powers to inspire awe and respect, she became a mean-spirited, more unpleasant character over the centuries.

In her more recent form, she is a witch who can turn herself into a bird, generally thought to be the striped cuckoo, although some say a barn owl. In this form, she flies onto the roofs of houses at night and makes dreadful screeching and squawking noises so that the people inside cannot get any sleep. She only stops this commotion if they offer her a gift—usually coffee or tobacco—and flies away.

The following day, she arrives at the same house, this time in her human form, to collect the promised gift. If it is not forthcoming, she curses them with the promise of disease or death.

This witchy Matinta Pereira is believed to be a hereditary malediction passed from mother to daughter. If there is no heiress to this horrible hex, she can try to pass it on if she can find someone to agree. Vain and greedy women are at particular risk of being tricked into taking this responsibility.

Villages determined to rid themselves of Matinta Pereira have a special ritual. A key must be buried near where she is expected to appear. Scissors are placed over the earth, covering it, along with a rosary (for best results, each bead should be separately blessed). When Matinta Pereira walks over it, her spirit will be trapped, and her curse must be swept away with a broom to ensure it will not fester.

Pisadeira ("Stamping Woman") is another witch-like entity. She is described as a hag with the eyes of the devil. She is best known in the Minas Gerais region, particularly in São Paulo.

She has the horrible, cackling laugh synonymous with witches and has a foul and putrid odor about her. Physically, she has a big nose, a turned-up chin, and a twisted, wide mouth. She can be skinny or fat. She is often depicted with long, bony fingers and is dressed in tatty rags, sometimes with a red cap.

She climbs upon rooftops, searching for greedy people who have gone to bed with full stomachs after eating too much. When she finds one, she climbs onto them so they cannot breathe.

Pisadeira was used to explain the phenomenon of sleep paralysis and has similarities to the concept of the incubus, which is said to cause nightmares and night terrors among Europeans. Pisadeira was the subject of some verses by the celebrated Brazilian poet Cora Coralina (a nom de plume of Anna Lins dos Guimarães Peixoto Bretas). "The Pisadeira comes, won't let you sleep, and in the morning, you are broken like hell."

Folklorists believe Pisadeira might have developed from the Portuguese mythical character Fradinho da Mão Furado. He is a friar who disturbs sleepers. When they awake, he presses his hands on their chests to stop them from screaming.

Chapter Eight – African Influences

In Brazilian mythology, several legends can be traced back to early Portuguese and Moorish stories. For instance, stories of beautiful princesses who are cursed in order to guard treasure hoards and stories of snake princesses have permeated the folklore of northern Brazil.

In the Middle Ages, the North African Muslim people (often referred to as the Moors) were frequently in conflict with the Europeans in the Iberian Peninsula. For seven hundred years, the Arabian and Moorish forces had a presence in the region and were only defeated in Spain as the Age of Exploration began in 1492.

The presence of the Moors made a deep impact on Iberian culture, particularly in literature and architecture, but with their defeat and the creation of the modern countries of Spain and Portugal, the Moors were treated with disdain and enslaved for cheap labor and frequently shipped across the Atlantic to help build the new colonies in South America.

Jericoacoara, in the municipality of Jijoca, Ceará, has a lighthouse. It is said that beneath it, closed off by huge iron gates, lies a wonderful city full of beauty and riches. However, the gates of this city are guarded by a huge serpent with golden scales and the head and feet of a woman, an enchanted princess called Carolina, the *Princesa Encantada de Jericoacoara*.

Her curse can only be lifted after a human sacrifice has been performed immediately outside the city's gates. Some of the blood from that unfortunate has to be painted along her scaly back. Then, she will become the beautiful princess she was, her marvelous city of riches will open, and she will marry her rescuer (who has a questionable character, having just slaughtered an innocent person on a somewhat sketchy premise). This hero will become lord and king of her realm.

Another of these enduring myths that is believed to have its roots in the arrival of the Portuguese colonists is the story of Teiniaguá, another Moorish princess.

The beautiful Teiniaguá managed to escape the brutal attention of her Spanish oppressors and fled to the south of Brazil. There, she encountered Anghangá, who promptly cursed her. She became a salamander with a gleaming ruby on her head. She is destined to remain in a lagoon in the Jarau crater in the Paraná Basin, Rio Grande do Sul.

In the nearby small town of São Tomé, there was a young sacristan who served the priests at the church. He visited the lagoon, and when he saw the salamander, he captured it in a bull horn and took it back to his lodgings at the church.

In another version of Teiniaguá's story, the sacristan was distracted by a bubbling sound that seemed to come from the heart of the lagoon. The noise seemed to become louder and louder until he felt sure the whole lake was being boiled. Then, an unearthly light from beneath the water began to grow brighter and rise in a ball as if to head for him. Terrified, the sacristan tried to flee but found he was unable to move. Suddenly, in a flash, the light transformed into a jeweled salamander with a ruby on its head. The young man quickly captured it in a bull horn and took it back to his lodgings at the church.

He remembered hearing an old story about an enchanted lizard that, if treated well, would guide a good man to a cave full of treasure. He wondered if the tale might be true. He carefully opened the horn, ready to feed the salamander, when there was a blinding flash. A lovely young woman stepped out of the horn and grew larger and larger until it was clear she was human.

The sacristan had never seen such perfection before and wondered whether he had captured a goddess at the lagoon. He fell to his knees in awe, and then, turning to him, she spoke. She told him that she had been cursed by a foul demon and explained that she was an unfortunate princess. When the sacristan tried to apologize for his humble surroundings that ill befitted her beauty and status, she laughed softly. As he looked around, his spartan room had become furnished with the richest, most exotic furnishings. The dark walls now glistened with sparkling light as though they were embedded with gemstones and pearls, and the air was scented with sweet and heady perfume.

Teiniaguá then told the astonished young man that she would be his lover. The two spent the night together in his enchanted room, but in the morning, she disappeared. The poor sacristan was exhausted and devastated. He looked dreadful with his tired, red eyes and found it difficult to concentrate on his work, worrying the priests. They wondered what could be the matter with their young attendant who was usually so diligent.

For his part, the sacristan was concerned about his sins and longed to confess, but he could not bring himself to betray Teiniaguá. That night, when he retired to his room, she returned, and they loved each other again. From then on, she came to him every night.

One evening, Teiniaguá asked the sacristan to let her taste the communion wine. Unable to refuse his beloved, they went to the church and drank chalice after chalice of the sacred wine. After making love by the altar, they fell asleep.

The next morning, the sacristan awoke, but he was not alone. The priests found him surrounded by the trappings of his debauchery, but Teiniaguá, as usual, had disappeared. The townspeople were appalled at his behavior, and since he refused to say who he had been with in the church, he was sentenced to death. The young man was crippled by shame and guilt, but he was even more devastated at the thought of never seeing his princess again.

A crowd gathered to watch his execution. Suddenly, a bolt of lightning came as if from nowhere, and a shining figure rose from the lagoon. Teiniaguá, shimmering in her beauty, appeared before the crowd, who ran away terrified. She turned to the sacristan and led him away to the caves of Cerro do Jarau, where they remained for two hundred years, guarding the fabled treasure there.

However, this enchantment was not permanent. It could be broken if someone completed seven specific trials. When this person was granted a wish, they could ask for the treasure and the couple guarding it to be freed. After two centuries had passed, a man completed these trials but asked for nothing in return. As he left, the sacristan gave the champion a golden coin.

A few days passed, and the man heard that one of his neighbors was selling his herd of cattle, so he went to buy himself a bull. He picked up the golden coin, and to his surprise, it multiplied and continued to multiply until he had enough coins to buy the whole herd.

News quickly spread, and people wondered how this man, who was known to be poor, had managed to afford the cattle. They concluded that he must have made a pact with the devil. They refused to trade with him and ostracized him. Soon, he could bear it no longer and returned the herd to his neighbor in exchange for the enchanted golden coin, which he took back to the cave.

When he gave it back to the sacristan, the curse was broken. Teiniaguá and her sacristan left the cave and settled in Rio Grande do Sul, where the people of Iberian-Amerindian heritage are said to be their descendants.

There are many myths and legends in Brazil's canon that undeniably have their origins in the shameful period of slavery.

São Luis is the capital and largest city of the state of Maranhão, home to the indigenous Tupinambá people. It has an interesting history, particularly since it was founded in 1612 by a French naval officer and then swiped by the Portuguese three years later. It was also under Dutch occupation between 1641 and 1644. In recent times, it has become the heart of reggae in Brazil and has a vibrant and popular culture.

São Luis is also home to the ghostly story of Ana Jansen's carriage. In the dead of night, an antiquated rattling carriage hurtles through the streets. It is pulled by headless horses and guided by a coachman, who also is missing a head. If that wasn't enough, the clatter of the carriage is accompanied by wails of tormented souls or the squealing of gears in need of oiling.

Inside the carriage is the heavily veiled Ana Jansen, whom no one has quite managed to see. In life, she was said to be an evil slave owner who meted out cruel punishments for no reason at all. Her haunting is an attempt to atone for her wickedness, as she implores passersby to pray for her soul from inside her darkened carriage.

Ana Jansen was a real person. In the 19th century, she was banished from the family home when it was discovered she was pregnant. She then had a love affair with Colonel Isidoro Pereira, the wealthiest man in the province. He had made a fortune from his cotton and sugar plantations, where enslaved African workers provided the heavy labor.

When he died, Ana Jansen took over his business interests and was very successful, so much so that Dom Pedro II, Emperor of Brazil, called her the "Queen of Maranhão." Though it is certainly true that she had more enslaved workers than anyone else in the region, there is no tangible evidence that she was any crueler than any other slave owner.

Even in her lifetime, there were rumors of her cruelty and wickedness. She was said to have had numerous affairs with prominent figures to increase her wealth and status. She was supposed to have poisoned the town's water supply by throwing dead cats in the wells so that the townspeople were forced to buy water from her.

Her supposed treatment of slaves was incredibly brutal. She would have them prostrate themselves face down on the ground so she could walk on them to save her shoes from getting muddy in rainy weather. Any enslaved person she considered disobedient or too pretty would be flung into a pit of spikes. It was said the people of Maranhão hated her. A merchant saw this as a business opportunity. He ordered a large number of *penicos* (a chamber pot) bearing an image of her face at the bottom. Ana Jansen heard about this and quietly sent her staff to buy all of them. Days later, this merchant opened his front door to find every *penico* had been left there. They were full of human excrement.

There seems to be little doubt that her reputation was embellished or even completely made up. This myth serves as a good example of women being vilified for their successes.

There is a legend about the procession of the dead that shares elements of Ana Jansen's story. It concerns a nosey old woman who spent her time at her window spying on her neighbors for anything she could gossip about. She was well known for her uncharitable behavior and spiteful ways.

One Ash Wednesday, late at night, she was at her window, as usual, when she saw a procession of hooded figures slowly making their way through the street. She knew the church had not planned any such procession, and in any case, it was far too late for such activities. Despite this, she remained glued to the window, desperate to know what was going on.

As the figures passed her home, one of the figures handed her a candle, and then they were gone. With no more to see, the old woman went to bed, but the next morning, she went to pick up the candle, only to find it was a human bone. Needless to say, she realized the folly of her ways and never snooped or gossiped again.

Some believe this procession of spirits that walk at midnight are the spirits of the African people brought to South America by the Europeans who never saw their families or homelands again. Because of this, their lives are unfinished, and they need to march to get some kind of closure before their souls can move on to the next world.

The procession is also thought to be a portent of death. The leader of the ghostly marchers is said to knock on the door of the next person in the community who will die.

In the tradition of haunted floating body parts that pervade Brazilian mythology, there is a disembodied hand with black hairy skin. This mythical presence is believed to materialize mostly in the southeastern regions of Brazil and is especially prevalent in São Paulo. It is known as Mãozinha-Preta ("Little Black Hand") or Mãozinha-da-Justiça ("Little Hand of Justice"), and it is thought to be the spirit of an African enslaved person brought to Brazil.

Its reason for existence is to help protect African Brazilians from racist attacks and to mete out justice if any of them are hurt. It will pinch, slap, or strike anyone it perceives to be a threat to those it protects.

In the age of slavery, exhausted Black laborers could call on the hand for help when they were overwhelmed by work, knowing it would never harm them. In one story, a greedy slave owner called upon it to do the work of some of his workers, and it reluctantly agreed. But when the slave owner ordered it to beat his slaves, it turned on him in anger and beat him within an inch of his life. He was lucky; some say Mãozinha-Preta will strangle its enemies.

Chapter Nine – Folktales and Fairytales

The Brazilian story of Domingo's cat has strong similarities to the European Puss in Boots, Dick Whittington, and Aladdin from the *Arabian Nights*.

Domingo was a young man who had a cat that he adored. He was poor and would gladly sacrifice his own needs to ensure his cat was fed.

One day, his cat told him not to worry anymore because he was taking control and would make their fortune. He went into the forest and dug a hole. He found five pieces of silver. He bought some food for himself and Domingo and then took the rest of the silver to the king.

The next day, the cat went back to the forest and dug up several pieces of gold, which he took to the king as well. On the third day, he dug up diamonds and gifted them to the king.

By then, the king had started to ask who was giving him these fine gifts, and the cat was presented to him. The cat told him that they were from his master, Domingo.

The king thought that this Domingo must be extremely wealthy and a potential husband for his lovely daughter. He asked the cat to bring Domingo to the palace so they could arrange a marriage.

When the cat told Domingo, he protested that he couldn't possibly marry the princess. What could he possibly wear? The cat told him not to worry, and he returned to the royal palace. He told the king that there had been a terrible fire where Domingo's clothes were made and kept, and his tailors had burned to death. He asked the king if Domingo could borrow something suitable. The king, sympathetic in the face of this calamity, loaned Domingo one of his finest costumes.

Domingo put it on and looked just like a noble prince, but he was still concerned. Where would he and the princess live?

The cat told him not to worry and traveled through the forest to a mountain where a giant lived in a palace. The cat politely asked the giant to loan this fine palace to his master, but the giant was outraged at the request and refused. The cat promptly turned the giant into a mouse and then killed and ate him.

Domingo and the princess were married and sailed down the river on a magnificent barge to the giant's palace. It was filled with riches beyond their wildest dreams. Domingo turned to his cat to thank him for all he had done, but he had gone.

The mysterious, clever, and wise cat had gone to bring good fortune to someone else who valued him beyond all else. Domingo never forgot him, and he lived a long and happy life with his princess.

In a story that explains how pigeons became tame, a father had three sons ready to leave home and make their way in the world. He gave each of them a large melon with the warning only to open them by water.

In fairytale tradition, the brothers each took a different path. It was a hot day, and the eldest opened his melon as soon as he had left so he wouldn't have to carry it. To his amazement, a beautiful young woman stepped out of the fruit and asked him for water or milk. The young man had neither, and she fell to her knees and died.

The second son had chosen a path that took him uphill. He quickly became hot and tired. He soon became unbearably thirsty and broke his melon, eager for some of the juice inside. Just as before, another lovely maiden stepped out of it, asking for water or milk. He, too, was unable to provide either, and she died there and then.

The third brother was finding his journey just as difficult. The terrain was difficult, and he grew tired and thirsty, but he did not forget his father's advice. He continued to carry the heavy, cumbersome fruit.

Eventually, he reached a town where he saw a fountain. After taking a drink himself, he opened his melon, and a beautiful woman stepped out. As soon as she asked, he gave her some water, and then she hid in a nearby tree while he went to find some food for them.

As she waited, she watched the townspeople coming to the fountain for their water. A pretty little enslaved Black girl carrying a large pot on her head couldn't resist admiring her reflection in the water. As she gazed upon her own face, she thought to herself that she shouldn't be carrying water for her lazy old mistress and threw the pot to the ground, smashing it into thousands of pieces.

However, when she returned without the pot or water, she was whipped as a punishment and sent out again with a new water jar. As she bent to fill it, she heard the young woman in the tree laughing softly. Realizing that her moment of vanity must have been seen by someone, she angrily took a pin from her pinafore and plunged it into the woman in the tree. When its sharp point pierced her skin, she transformed into a pigeon.

The young man returned, and the Black maid, terrified, hid herself in the branches of the tree. When he saw her, he couldn't understand what had happened, but the little maid quickly told him that she had been badly sunburned while she had waited for him. Satisfied, he took her with him, and they got married.

However, the young man always felt uneasy about his bride, and her sunburn never faded. Over the years, he became very wealthy, and he bought a grand house for his family, with a magnificent garden that became his pride and joy. He delighted in the exotic, perfumed plants he could grow, and birds came from far and wide to sing in this special place. As the man sauntered along his garden paths, a pigeon always seemed to follow him. The bird constantly flew around him, which he found very irritating.

When his wife fell sick, he ordered that this pigeon should be cooked for her. As it was being roasted, the cook noticed something was embedded in the bird's breast. None of the kitchen staff could pull it out. She called to the master, and he was easily able to pull the pin from the pigeon. Instantly, it transformed into the lovely maiden who had come from the melon.

Faced with this woman, the man's wife wept as she admitted what she had done and then (conveniently) died. The melon woman and the man married and had a long and happy life, but she always remembered her life as a pigeon. Until then, these birds had always lived deep in the forests and away from the towns. She had little houses built in the garden so that they could nest there. In time, families of pigeons saw the houses and nested in them, laying their eggs and raising their chicks in that beautiful greenery.

From then on, pigeons (according to the story) became accustomed to living alongside people and left the forests to nest in the cities of Brazil.

The manioca, or cassava plant, is a woody shrub native to South America. Its starchy root is one of the pillars of Brazilian cuisine and can be used in several different ways. It can be used much like a potato, it can be dried and ground into flour, and it has proven health benefits.

The myth of how it came to be has been passed down through the generations. Once upon a time, the daughter of an important chief found she was pregnant. She had never had a relationship before and could not explain how it had happened, but her father did not believe her. He punished her cruelly, demanding to know the identity of her baby's father. However, she couldn't tell him; she truly had no idea how it had happened.

After nine months had passed, she gave birth to the most astonishing child. This little girl, named Mani, could walk and talk before she was a year old. Her sunny disposition endeared her to everyone.

Then, suddenly, with no explanation, Mani died. The community was distraught, and the chief of the village insisted that she should be buried in his home near where he slept.

Soon afterward, a strange plant began to grow from her grave, and a spirit came to the chief in his dreams. It told him to dig up the plant for the root, which would bring sustenance and good health to his people. He did this, and the cassava has since become a staple in people's diets.

There are several stories about the animals of the jungle. Many are in the tradition of explaining why they have certain characteristics, such as why the toad has bruised skin and how the rabbit lost its tail. Monkeys have more than their fair share of these folktales. The most well known of these monkey tales explains why they believe bananas belong to them.

An old woman had a marvelous garden in which she grew bananas that were the envy of everyone who saw them. Because she was old and not strong or agile enough to climb up the trees to harvest the fruit, she asked the biggest monkey to do it in return for half of what she had grown.

This monkey set to work and did as he had been asked. However, when he finished, he took all the ripe large bananas as his half and left the old woman with the smaller, tougher fruit that grew at the bottom of the trees.

The old woman was furious that she had been tricked and resolved to get her revenge on the big monkey. After a great deal of thought, she made a little boy from wax and put a basket on top of his head so he looked just like a peddler. Then, she found the plumpest, sweetest, and yellowest bananas and arranged them in the basket.

Soon enough, the big monkey passed the little wax boy and saw the tempting bananas. In his most wheedling, pitiful voice, the monkey begged the boy for a banana. Of course, the wax boy said nothing.

The big monkey wasn't used to being ignored and angrily said he would push him if he wouldn't give him a banana. Still, the wax boy stayed silent, so the big monkey gave him a sharp push with his right forepaw.

His paw sank into the wax and stuck firm. The monkey was furious and demanded the wax boy release him immediately and give him two bananas. Otherwise, he would push him again. The boy gave no response, so the monkey pushed him again.

With both forepaws stuck in the wax, the big monkey was burning with rage and kicked the boy so that his hind paws were also stuck. He roared and howled until almost every monkey in the forest came to see what terrible calamity had befallen the biggest monkey.

The littlest monkey had the idea that they should all climb on top of each other into a huge pyramid, with the loudest monkey at the top, so he could call out to the sun and ask for help.

The sun was sympathetic to the biggest monkey's plight and sent its hottest rays to melt the wax until the biggest monkey could pull his paws free.

The poor old woman was aghast to see the sun helping the monkeys. They laughed, cheered, and made rude gestures at her. She could see there was no point in her continuing to remain there. She left her banana garden to the jubilant monkeys and moved a long way away. She grew cabbages in her new home.

The colorful wing cases of the beetles of Brazil are explained in a fable similar to Aesop's tale of the tortoise and the hare. It begins at the time when all beetles were brown. A grey rat saw a little female brown beetle making slow but steady progress as it walked along a wall. The rat mocked it for its lack of speed.

The rat showed her how fast it could dart and scurry, but she barely looked, instead continuing on her way. A blue and gold parrot that had been watching with interest from its perch flew down and suggested that if they raced, it would provide a new coat in whatever bright colors the winner wanted, courtesy of its friend, the tailor bird.

The drab little beetle and the dull grey rat found this prospect irresistible. Both dreamed of a glow-up. The rat boasted that he would soon have orange stripes like a tiger, as he was certain he would win.

When the race began, the little beetle started determinedly. The rat saw the laborious progress she was making and saw no point in rushing, but when he reached the finish line, the little beetle was waiting there for him. "How could this be?" he wondered.

The little beetle explained that she had decided to fly. The rat hadn't realized that she had wings and accepted he had been beaten. The parrot was as good as its word, and the little beetle was given a beautiful coat of green that sparkled with gold in the sunlight.

For a long time, beetles were delighted with these green coats until, one day, another little beetle longed to be as blue as the summer sky. She went to the tailor bird and begged him to make her an azure coat.

The tailor bird agreed but told her she would have to lose something. The little beetle agreed readily. When the coat was made, it was even more beautiful than the little beetle had imagined, with gleaming silver sparkles. She put it on and quickly realized what she had lost. It was soft rather than lacquer-hard like her green and gold coat had been, and from then on, she never grew again. This is why the blue beetles of Brazil are much smaller than their cousins.

This story finishes with the Brazilian flag. It is suggested that the background is the emerald green of the first beetle's coat, and the yellow diamond is its golden sheen. Within that is a blue circle that represents the earth. It is thought this represents the smaller beetles, and the white stars are just like the silver sparkles that enhance its coat. Underneath is Brazil's motto, "Ordem e Progresso" ("Order and Progress"), words that the wise little beetle might have called out when she raced the rat.

Conclusion

Despite the varied and extraordinary creation myths handed down through the generations, there is a notable lack of eschatological myths unique to Brazil that have survived, assuming they ever existed. There is, of course, the Armageddon and Day of Judgment in the Christian tradition. Catholicism is still the most widely practiced religion in Brazil (in 2020, 54.2 percent of the population identified as Catholic).

This lack of concern about the end of days is probably due to the fundamental belief in renewal and regeneration and a strong sense of spirituality. Death is accepted as a part of existence in most of the indigenous belief systems, but through social and sexual reproduction, it is accepted that society will continue and evolve as it always has. Remembering ancestors and heritage is important, and shared community stories help to fulfill this need. Beyond death, the spirit worlds are vague and beyond the grasp of humans (although some shamans are thought to be closer to understanding these secrets), and this belief has served to help build a strong and secure society with shared values and cultures.

The mythology of Brazil gives us an insight into the beliefs, values, and cultures of societies that once existed and continue to develop in this large, diverse part of South America. These stories teach life lessons that are often still relevant today.

Through the centuries, those people who have lived in Brazil celebrated their ancestors and reared their children in the same traditions, demonstrating a better understanding and respect for their environment. They were far better able to balance their existence than later, more sophisticated cultures that invaded and colonized with little regard for the future and the earth.

It is noticeable that many of these stories are concerned with protecting the natural world and punishing those who seek to destroy it. Mãe do Ouro ("Gold Mother"), for example, is an entity devoted to stopping the destruction of the landscape for that most desirable of natural elements, gold. Her presence has been recorded in the gold-rich states in the southeastern, northeastern, and central western regions of Brazil since the gold rushes of the 18th century, particularly in Mato Grosso, Goiás, and Minas Gerais. She is powerful and determined, ensuring those searching for gold cannot exploit the country's mines. Some say that anyone who rests their eyes on her will not live to tell the tale.

There are a lot of details about her appearance. She is beautiful and very fair, and she wears a long white gown that reflects the sunshine, giving her an aura of gleaming brightness. She can transform into a fireball when the need arises.

Her presence indicates that there are gold deposits nearby, and some gold prospectors believe she might lead them there if she believes they can be trusted to take just enough for their personal fortunes and promise never to reveal the location to anyone else.

Sometimes, Mão do Ouro is considered a guardian of wronged women, those beaten or abused by their husbands and living in misery. She is thought to lure these unpleasant men to a cave far from their homes, and there they remain for the rest of their lives while she finds good men who will treat their widows with decency and respect.

The beautiful archipelago of Fernando de Noronha, which lies off the northeastern coast of Brazil, is made up of twenty-one islands as a part of the State of Pernambuco. It is a major tourist destination and a UNESCO World Heritage Site. Its history is turbulent and fascinating. It has always had a limited population; in fact, it has been uninhabited at times and was a jail for Brazil's most dangerous criminals for long periods in the 18th, 19th, and 20th centuries.

These islands have several of their own myths and folktales that demonstrate the range and depth of Brazilian mythology and how these stories have been shaped by history. For example, there is a phantom gypsy woman who offers visitors cashew nuts. Her origin story is tied to the compulsory deportation of Romani people to Fernando de Noronha in 1739.

Another entity firmly linked to the islands' history is the headless priest who rides his white mule across the spectacular sun-bleached beaches at Quixaba. This is thought to be the spirit of Francisco Adelino de Brito Dantas, who discovered a source of drinking water for the grateful islanders. It is not certain why he lost his head and rides across the bay in death.

The spirit of a woman who was betrayed by her husband is said to live inside Morro do Pico, a mountain in Fernando de Noronha. A ravine will appear, in which a door will open, revealing a bright light. The spirit, in the form of a lovely woman, exits the door to find a young man to bring to the mountain with her. He will never be seen again, though his faint screams can be heard for several days.

Alamoa, who was once queen of the archipelago, is another seductress. She is unhappy with the islands being inhabited. She wanders as a stunning young woman around her former kingdom, looking for men to ensnare. Once she has their attention, they are lost. She either takes them to the top of Morro do Pico, where they feel compelled to jump to their deaths, or she traps them in her cave. Once there, she returns to her natural state—a rotting skeleton—and the men die of fright.

Unlike the other female spirit of the mountain, she cannot bear light. Some of the prisoners held in the island jail recounted how they would see her before a storm. She seemed to be dancing, suspended in the night air, and completely naked.

Her name is thought to come from the Portuguese *alemã*, meaning "German woman," and she is supposed to be blonde and blue-eyed with very fair skin. However, it is more likely that she was originally a character from a Dutch tale. They briefly occupied northeastern Brazil in the 1600s.

These stories serve as a microcosm of Brazilian mythology. These tales take elements from the oral traditions of the indigenous tribes, details from real events, and moral or cautionary messages. They blend the natural world with the spiritual world, showing the importance of both worlds in everyday life.

If you enjoyed this book, a review on Amazon would be greatly appreciated because it would mean a lot to hear from you.

To leave a review:
1. Open your camera app.
2. Point your mobile device at the QR code.
3. The review page will appear in your web browser.

Thanks for your support!

Here's another book by Enthralling History that you might like

Free limited time bonus

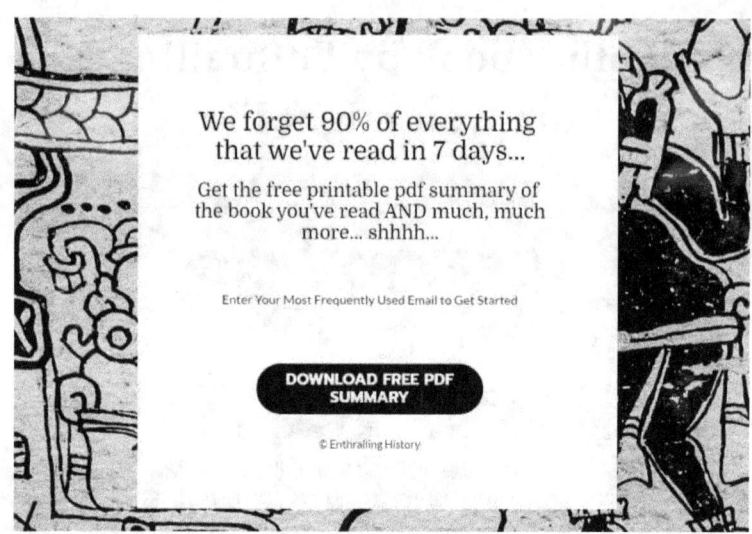

Stop for a moment. We have a free bonus set up for you. The problem is this: we forget 90% of everything that we read after 7 days. Crazy fact, right? Here's the solution: we've created a printable, 1-page pdf summary for this book that you're reading now. All you have to do to get your free pdf summary is to go to the following website: https://livetolearn.lpages.co/enthrallinghistory/

Or, Scan the QR code!

Once you do, it will be intuitive. Enjoy, and thank you!

Further Reading

Bierhorst, John
The Mythology of South America (1988)
Ardagh, Philip
South American Myths and Legends (1998)
Parker, Victoria
Traditional Tales from South America (2001)
Eells, Elsie Spicer
Fairy Tales from Brazil: How and Why Tales from Brazilian Folklore (2002)
Silva, Murilo Fidelis
Into the Wild: A Brief Journey into the Heart of Brazilian Folklore Legends (2023)
Cuscudo, Mario
Legends of the Amazon: Exploring Brazilian Mythology (2023)
Storm, Rachel and Carter, Geraldine
The Illustrated Guide to Latin American Mythology (1995)
Dorson, Mercedes and Wilmot, Jane
Tales from the Rain Forest: Myths and Legends from the Amazonian Indians of Brazil (1997)

www.ingramcontent.com/pod-product-compliance
Lightning Source LLC
Chambersburg PA
CBHW070228270426
43912CB00004B/56